**In No Time** ――――――――――――

Outlook
2000

# In No Time

# Outlook 2000

## Giesbert Damaschke

AN IMPRINT OF PEARSON EDUCATION

PEARSON EDUCATION LIMITED

**Head Office:**
Edinburgh Gate
Harlow CM20 2JE
Tel: +44 (0) 1279 623623
Fax: +44 (0) 1279 431059

**Head Office:**
128 Long Acre
London WC2E 9AN
Tel: +44 (0) 171 447 2000
Fax: +44 (0) 171 240 5771

First published in Great Britain 2000
© Pearson Education Limited 2000

First published in 1999 as *Outlook 2000: leicht, klar, sofort*
by Markt & Technik Buch- und Software-Verlag GmbH
Martin-Kollar-Straße 10–12
D-81829 Munich
GERMANY

*Library of Congress Cataloging in Publication Data*
Available from the publisher.

*British Library Cataloguing in Publication Data*
A CIP catalogue record for this book can be obtained from the British Library.

## ISBN 0-130-16229-9

Translated and typeset by Cybertechnics, Sheffield.                    •
Printed and bound in Great Britain by Henry Ling Ltd at The Dorset Press, Dorchester, Dorset.

*The publishers' policy is to use paper manufactured from sustainable forests.*

# Contents

## 5 The calendar 114

## 6 Contacts 156

# 7 Setting up e-mail 178

# 8 Working with e-mail 200

# 9 Notes 230

## 13 Organising and classifying ___ 292

# Dear Reader

Computers are useful appliances. Without complaining they process almost any amount of data we present to them; and yet they store even the smallest bit of information for as long as we want them to. Today they are probably the most important tool for the execution of your daily office work.

Unfortunately, computers do not only process information and data, they also produce both to a surprising extent. If you attempt to put the concept of the paperless office into practice, you are soon subjected to a flood of digital data from your computer, which produces non-stop memos, notes, appointments, and electronic mail.

If you do not want to drown in this flood of data, you will need help: Outlook 2000 can provide the required help. The program enables you to sail safely and confidently through the floods and to fish for any piece of information from the ocean of data. With Outlook you can manage your appointments, tasks, extensive contact entries and folders, your e-mails, groupwork, and so on.

Outlook is a versatile and flexible program. Its options are best learnt by constantly working with the software. This book aims to assist you in getting to know all the features and to ease your way into Outlook as naturally as possible.

Before you start, let me thank you. Not only for purchasing the book, but also for reading the introduction. (This is usually skipped and I'm not surprised).

I also want to thank Nina Krauß and Georg Weiherer, who have worked with the manuscript and have ensured that a collection of printed paper actually became a book.

And now: have fun with Outlook 2000.

Giesbert Damaschke

The following three pages show you how your computer keyboard is structured. Groups of keys are dealt with one by one to make it easier to understand.

Most of the computer keys are operated exactly as keys on a typewriter. However, there are a few additional keys, which are designed for the peculiarities of computer work.

See for yourself ......

# Typewriter keys

Use these keys exactly as you would on a typewriter.
The Enter key is also used to send commands to your computer.

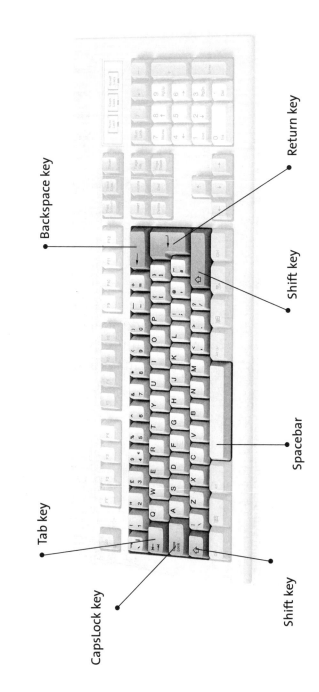

Backspace key

Return key

Shift key

Tab key

Spacebar

CapsLock key

Shift key

3

# Special keys, function keys, status lights, numeric key pad

Special keys and function keys are used for special tasks in computer operation. Ctrl-, Alt- and AltGr keys are usually used in combination with other keys. The Esc key can cancel commands, Insert and Delete can be used, amongst other things, to insert and delete text.

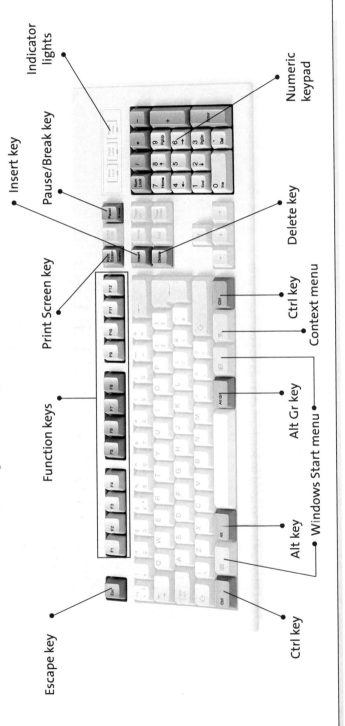

Escape key

Function keys

Print Screen key

Pause/Break key

Insert key

Indicator lights

Numeric keypad

Delete key

Ctrl key

Context menu

Alt Gr key

Windows Start menu

Alt key

Ctrl key

# Navigation keys

These keys are used to move around the screen.

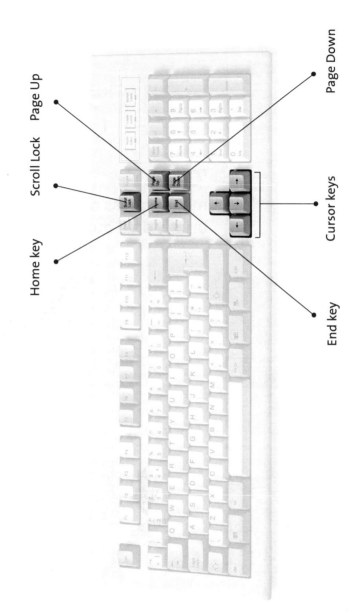

Scroll Lock · Page Up

Home key

Page Down

Cursor keys

End key

## 'Click ...'

means: press once
briefly on a button.

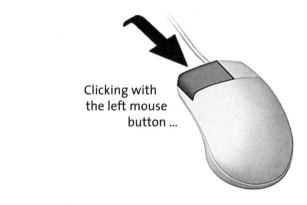

Clicking with
the left mouse
button ...

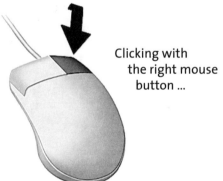

Clicking with
the right mouse
button ...

## 'Double-click ...'

means: press the left button
twice briefly in quick
succession

Double-clicking

## 'Drag ...'

means: click an object with the left
mouse button, keep the button
pressed, move the mouse and thus
drag the item to another position.

Drag

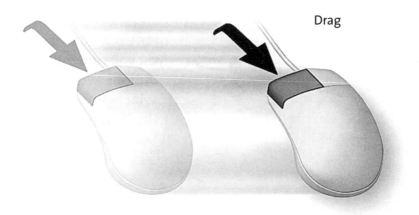

7

# 1

The first time

## What's in this chapter:

It is said that the best way to learn to swim is to jump in at the deep end. You may or may not agree. However, where computer programs are concerned there is some truth in it. At least you will not be in danger of drowning. Learning by doing is the motto. Thus, in this chapter we will simply play around with some functions of Outlook 2000 to see what happens. Do not worry: you cannot do any damage. The chapter will teach you how to start and end the program, but most of all you will find out what Outlook actually is and which problems or tasks you can tackle with the program.

## You are going to learn about:

# What is Outlook?

'Third time lucky' is a saying that seems to apply particularly well to Microsoft, as they usually have their big breakthrough with the third version of their programs. This was true with MS-DOS, Windows, and Word (even though the third version has been launched as version 6.0 on the market). If there still were the old system of counting versions, the new Outlook 2000 would also bear the number 3: In 1997 'Outlook', then followed 'Outlook 98', and now there is with 'Outlook 2000' – so to speak – Outlook 3.0.

As might be expected from a third version, Outlook is a mature and powerful program. The small imperfections of the preceding version have been corrected, the program has been extensively overhauled, and its integration with the other Office programs has generally been improved.

In a certain sense Outlook is the nerve centre of Office 2000. While Word or Excel are used for the execution of particular tasks – you write text in Word, and calculate spreadsheets in Excel – Outlook is used for managing, communicating, and structuring, operations which are essential to the execution of extensive tasks. What good is an excellent word processor like Word, if you do not know when to use it? With Word you write your report, and with Outlook you organise yourself to meet its deadline and get it to the address to which you have to send it.

This is a very simple example, but it will not be very difficult for you to think of many situations in your everyday office work – with all its appointments, notes, phone calls, meetings, memos, and conversations – in which you feel overwhelmed by the weight of tasks and information.

Outlook will help you to remain on top of everything. With Outlook you manage your **e-mail, appointments**, and **tasks**. In Outlook **phone numbers** and **addresses** of friends and acquaintances are always at hand, and so is much more.

So far you may still be able to do this with an appointments book, a few notes, and a little bit of patience. However, Outlook can do more.

Conventional scheduling and address management on paper will eventually reach a point at which you cannot find anything any more, however hard you may try. Before you even notice, notes you have just made disappear in a pile of entries, scraps of paper, and rubbish.

Yet we all have computers – why shouldn't the computer take care of managing this data (after all it produces most of it)? Computers may sometimes do funny things, but there is one thing they are perfect at: patiently storing and managing any single scrap of information.

As a computer program Outlook is incredibly patient. No matter what or how much information you store in Outlook – the program swallows almost every data dosage you administer. Best of all is that Outlook is able to retrieve everything you have ever entrusted to it at any time.

'Outlook' means 'view, sight'. Perhaps the developers at Microsoft have chosen the name because the consistent use of Outlook ensures order and a clear structure, and thus the perspective on the really important things and the context is not obstructed by unimportant trifles.

'Outlook' can also mean 'perspective, approach'. The program also lives up to this definition: Outlook offers the option to view the different kinds of information in different combinations.

Example: at first sight a business partner's address, an appointment, and a task are not connected. However, if the task is to send important documents to your business partner by a particular date, in Outlook the three entries form an important unit. To take full advantage of this, in Outlook it is possible to display the data in different views.

Outlook manages all data in a number of FOLDERS: these are like ring binders in which Outlook neatly files and stores the data. As it is intended to manage highly varied types of data, there is one folder for e-mails, one for notes, one for addresses, one for tasks, and so on.

Outlook not only replaces your appointments book, but also a whole filing cabinet full of ring binders.

Wait a minute; we are already into the structures and options of Outlook. It would be better to start at the beginning.

# Starting Outlook

Starting Outlook is very easy: like every other program under Windows 95/98, Outlook is started by clicking the START button (this makes sense, don't you think?). It probably does not make quite as much sense that you also close it via the START button, but that does not concern us here.

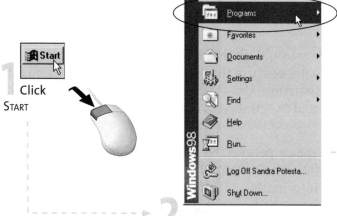

**1** Click
START

**2** The START menu opens. Choose the menu item PROGRAMS. You can click this item or just move the cursor onto it. In any case...

3 ...the PROGRAMS menu is going to open. Choose the MICROSOFT OUTLOOK entry and click it to start the program.

However, in Windows and in Outlook there are often many ways to reach the same goal. There is also a shortcut for starting Outlook. During the installation of Outlook a corresponding symbol is created on your desktop.

Microsoft Outlook

4 Double-clicking this symbol saves you using the longer way via the START menu.

Depending on your configuration you may be prompted to set up an e-mail account. However, we will deal with e-mail accounts, their management, and the question of what they actually are, later (see Chapters 7 and 8).

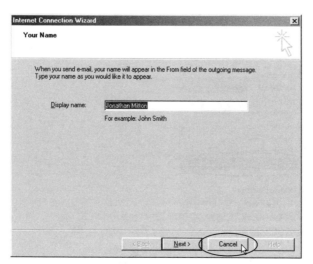

**5** At the moment the Internet Connection Wizard only confuses. Click on *Cancel* to get rid of it.

There is a final obstacle to overcome: the Office Assistant. Admittedly, it is supposed to help you to use Outlook, and the programmers designed it very well, but at the beginning it causes additional problems and confusion instead of helping.

**6** To switch off the bubbly if slightly annoying fellow, click it with the right mouse button

7 A small menu window opens (a so-called context menu). Here choose the HIDE ASSISTANT entry, and confirm by clicking it with the left mouse button.

# Outlook Today

Whichever way you have chosen to start Outlook, on your screen you will now see something very much like this:

This is how Outlook presents itself to you when it first starts up. Your screen may not look exactly like in the figure – Outlook offers a range of display options, so that your opening screen might look slightly different.

The main part of the screen is occupied by the 'Outlook Today' window. So let's deal with it first.

'**Outlook Today**' shows you the most important information at a glance.

Personal Folders - Outlook Today
16 July 1999

1 The current **date** ...

Calendar

**Today**
1:00 PM - 3:00 PM    Dentist

**Tuesday**
▶ 11:00 AM - 2:00 PM  Moving

2 ... today's and future **appoint-ments** ...

A small arrow always points to your next outstanding appointment. In this way you can always see at a glance how much you have already done and what is still to come. You might consider this to be merely a gadget, but it is an important optical signal. You will notice that these seemingly fanciful bits significantly facilitate orientation in the jumble of your daily appointments and tasks. Outlook possesses a range of these inconspicuous but very efficient signals and indicators.

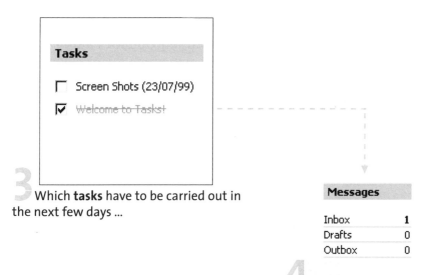

**3** Which **tasks** have to be carried out in the next few days ...

**Messages**

| | |
|---|---|
| Inbox | **1** |
| Drafts | 0 |
| Outbox | 0 |

**4** ....and an overview of the state of your **mailbox.**

Of course 'Outlook Today' does not only display information but also permits you to access it directly. When you move the mouse pointer across the individual elements of 'Outlook Today', you will notice that it keeps changing:

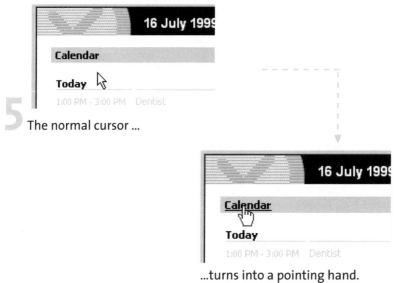

**5** The normal cursor ...

...turns into a pointing hand.

**17**

Furthermore the chosen item is underlined. These two changes mark the fact that you can activate the selected function with a single mouse click. Let's have a go.

# Entering an appointment

If you are already in 'Outlook Today', you might as well have a quick look at the calendar and the task list, and try to enter an appointment and a task.

This is how you do it:

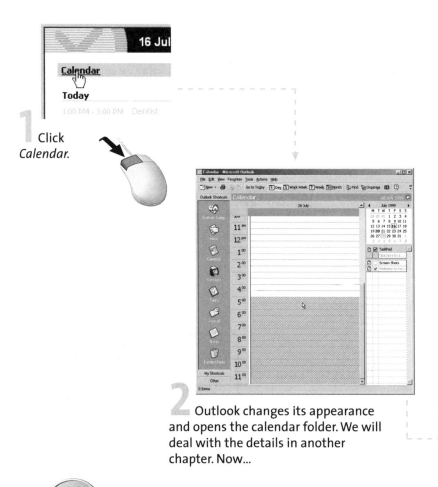

**1** Click *Calendar*.

**2** Outlook changes its appearance and opens the calendar folder. We will deal with the details in another chapter. Now...

**3** ...simply right-click on the sheet for the day.

**4** From the context menu choose the entry NEW AP-POINTMENT.

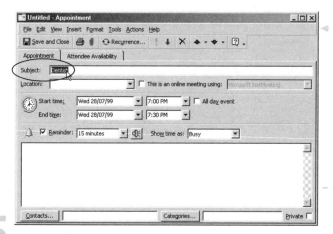

**5** An empty **appointment form**, which might appear slightly confusing at first glance, opens. However, do not be put off by the many buttons, symbols, and boxes, but enter what the appointment is for under Subject. In this example: an appointment at the dentist ...

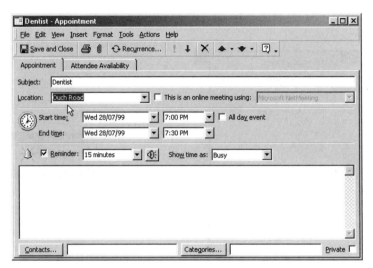

6 ...whose surgery is on 'Ouch Road'.

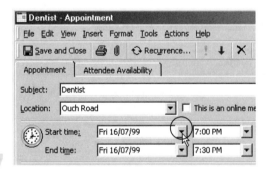

7 Of course every appointment has a beginning and an end. You specify these by clicking once the small arrow next to Start time...

8 ...and choosing the appropriate date from the calendar sheet (here Thursday, 29 April).

9 In the same way enter the time ...

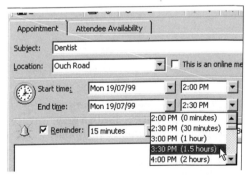

10 ...and how long the appointment will presumably take.

21

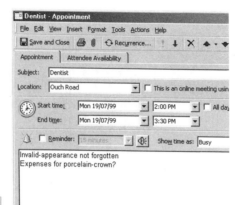

**11** Finally you can enter annotations to this appointment into the big empty box.

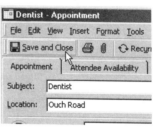

**12** By clicking the button *Save and Close* the appointment is entered into the calendar.

As the appointment is in the future, the calendar does not appear to have changed at first glance. However, if you look at the calendar preview in the top right corner you will notice that the 29 April is now displayed in **bold** script. This indicates that on this day you have one or more appointments.

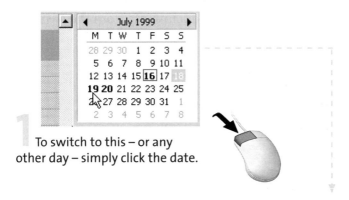

**1** To switch to this – or any other day – simply click the date.

**2** The daily view switches to the chosen day. As you can see, Outlook has correctly entered the appointment.

# Entering tasks

Usually an appointment does not appear out of thin air, but is more or less connected to your daily business affairs. Thus, you do not only have to remember to go to a meeting, but also to prepare for it, and to take along important documents; or sometimes you have to re-member to get a present and a card for a birthday.

In Outlook things like this are noted down on the task list, and this is why it is displayed together with the calendar. In our example (dentist) you have to remember to order documents from the NHS. You enter the task as follows:

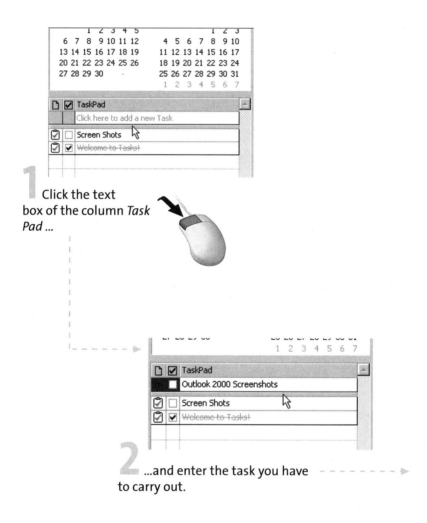

**1** Click the text box of the column *Task Pad* ...

**2** ...and enter the task you have to carry out.

**3** By pressing the ⏎ key the entry is added to the task list.

Now go to 'Outlook Today', by clicking the appropriate symbol in the left column. Outlook then displays the information that you do not only have a dentist appointment but that you also have to remember to take your documents. And that's exactly what Outlook is there for. Among other things.

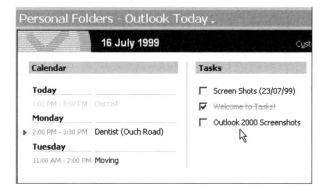

# Customising Outlook Today

One of the great advantages of Outlook is its almost limitless flexibility, which permits you to organise Outlook according to your wishes. For example here is how you can change 'Outlook Today'.

**25**

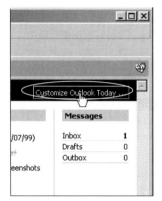

**1** To change the appearance of 'Outlook Today', select the *Customize Outlook Today* button (at the top right corner) ...

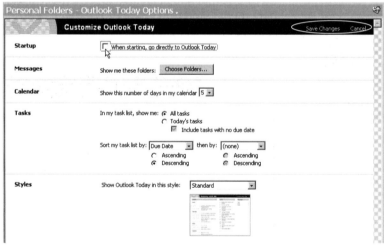

**2** ....and the display changes. Instead of the date you can now read 'Options'. The button with which you have switched into this area turns into *Save Changes* and *Cancel*.

Under it there are five areas in which you can make changes.

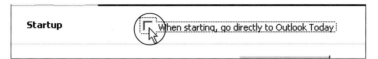

**3** Usually Outlook automatically switches into 'Outlook Today' at the first program start-up. If you do not want this to happen, you can switch off this function here. Outlook will then show your mailbox at program start-up.

**4** Outlook manages your e-mail in several folders. Here you can determine which mail folder you want Outlook to display at start-up. Usually you will not want to modify anything here. Thus, a perhaps somewhat cryptic description will do at this point.

**5** Under the options for 'Calendar' you can specify how many days in advance you want 'Outlook Today' to display your appointments. To change this setting, click once on the small arrow next to *Show this number of days in my calendar.*

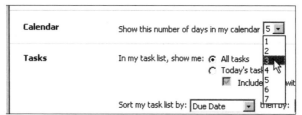

**6** A drop-down list opens, from which you can choose a number (of days) from 1 to 7.

How many days you want to be displayed in the calendar of 'Outlook Today' depends, of course, on how many appointments you have. If you have very many appointments you should only select one or two days, or else 'Outlook Today' might be insufficiently clear. If you have only a few appointments you can choose up to a week.

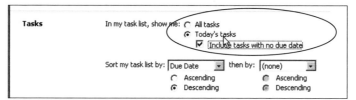

**7** The settings under 'Tasks' are quite complex. First determine whether you want to have 'All tasks' displayed or only those which are due on the current day.

As with the calendar settings, your **task settings** depend on how extensive your task list is. For very many tasks it is recommended to restrict the display to the tasks which are currently due, otherwise the clarity of 'Outlook Today' suffers.

| Tasks | In my task list, show me: ○ All tasks |
|---|---|
| | ⦿ Today's tasks |
| | ☑ Include tasks with no due date |

Sort my task list by: Due Date ▼ then by: (none) ▼
(none)
Importance ⬆
Due Date
Creation Time
Start Date

| Styles | Show Outlook Today in this style: Standard ▼ |

**8** Then you can determine two criteria according to which the tasks list will be sorted. Choose the first criterion from the left-hand menu (here the priority you can assign to a task) ...

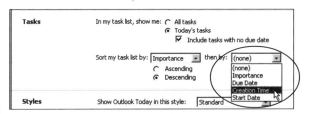

| Tasks | In my task list, show me: ○ All tasks |
|---|---|
| | ⦿ Today's tasks |
| | ☑ Include tasks with no due date |

Sort my task list by: Importance ▼ then by: (none) ▼
○ Ascending (none)
⦿ Descending Importance
Due Date
Creation Time ⬆
Start Date

| Styles | Show Outlook Today in this style: Standard |

**9** ...and select the second criterion from the right-hand menu (here the time at which the task has been entered). With these settings the most recent and most important entries are listed at the top.

Do not be put off by the setting options. Always remember that you can change them but you do not have to. Usually the default settings with which Outlook first starts are perfectly sufficient.

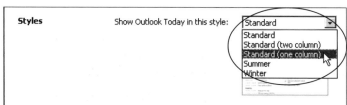

Styles         Show Outlook Today in this style:   Standard

Standard
Standard (two column)
Standard (one column)
Summer
Winter

**10** The last item specifies how Outlook arranges the various calendar, tasks, and messages areas of 'Outlook Today'. You have a choice between *Standard* (three columns), *Standard (two columns)* (the calendar takes up one column, and the tasks and messages share the other), *Standard (one column)* (calendar, tasks, and messages share one column), and the two options *Summer* and *Winter* which work with different colours and fonts. The space-saving display as one column is suitable for small screens. However, you had better try this for yourself.

**11** Now click
*Save changes.*

**12** Outlook switches back to Outlook Today, where you can examine the changes you have made.

# Exiting Outlook

In some programs you have to take care that you have closed all files and saved all changes before you close them. This does not apply to Outlook. You can exit the program at any time without having to worry about losing your data. Outlook saves all changes – whether they are entries in the various program folders or display options – and next time starts with the modified settings.

If you ever accidentally exit the program, you do not need to worry. Simply restart it, and you will find Outlook just as you had left it.

To exit the program there are – as for all Windows programs – two options.

1 You can click on the item FILE on the menu bar ...

2 ...and choose the entry EXIT from the open menu.

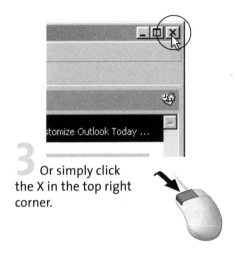

**3** Or simply click
the X in the top right
corner.

Both ways have the same effect: Outlook saves all data, closes all
open files, and exits.

**33**

The Outlook screen

## What's in this chapter:

Outlook 2000 is an extremely flexible program which may at first sight look intimidating and complicated. But do not fear: it just looks that way. After all, Outlook is supposed to help you to reduce your work, not cause additional problems. In this chapter, therefore, we will deal with all the individual elements of the Outlook screen in turn. Furthermore, we will find out which function is carried out by which part of the screen. You will see: in its basic structure Outlook is very straightforward.

**35**

# The structure of Outlook

Outlook is composed of various components, which are usually displayed next to each other in one window – however, as you will see later on, this is not necessarily so. Now start the program, so that we can have a closer look at the various areas and their functions.

Outlook is divided into **four areas:**

In the top area of the window you can find the **menu bar and the toolbars**, as you know them from other Office products. These bars, via which all functions of Outlook are controlled, can be placed and configured by you in any way you want.

On the left-hand side you can see the so-called '**Outlook bar**'. The somewhat cryptic name 'Outlook Links' will become clear later. Microsoft introduced this type of control element for the first time in Outlook. However, it is now also used in other Office programs and will probably play a central part in future Windows versions.

Most of the space is occupied by the area in which the actual information is dis-

played, in this case '**Outlook Today**' (so far – this will change soon).

Finally, at the bottom you can see the so-called 'status bar'. At the moment it is empty and not very spectacular, but later it will contain useful information.

# The menu bar

As almost every other Windows program Outlook 2000 also possesses a so-called 'menu bar'. This is the control centre via which all Outlook commands can be called up. All other elements such as the toolbar or the Outlook bar are thus in principle superfluous. However, they offer many shortcuts and options for some operations which via the menu bar can only be reached with great difficulty.

In the following we will briefly scroll through the **menu bar** to get a general overview of the Outlook options. The individual **menu entries** are only mentioned briefly. We will return to them at a different place.

Normally the menu bar is at the top of the window, but that is not necessarily so. You can place it underneath the toolbar, at either side or the bottom margins, and even outside the Outlook window. You do this as follows:

Move the cursor to the left margin of the menu bar until it changes into a four-sided arrow. Holding down the left mouse button ...

2 ...drag the bar into the position you want it to be.

3 Once you have placed the bar where you want it to be, simply release the mouse button – voilà.

4 If you want to move the menu bar back to its original position, simply double-click the margin and the bar automatically jumps back to where it came from.

No matter what you do with Outlook, the entries FILE, EDIT, VIEW, FAVORITES, TOOLS, OPERA-

TIONS, and HELP always remain the same. However, the individual menu items listed under these entries always depend on the respective situation. Thus, the menu may always look the same, but will certainly not always offer the same contents.

As there may be many rarely used items under any menu entry, Outlook 2000 works with a two-level system, the so-called personalised menu bars.

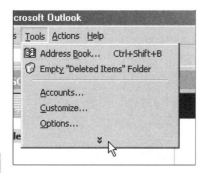

1 When you click a menu item, a menu opens as usual. However, in contrast to other menus it has a downward pointing double arrow as its last entry. When you click this arrow ...

**39**

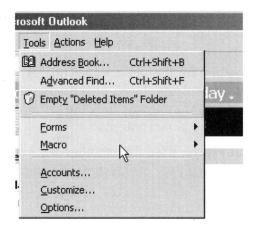

2 ...the chosen menu is extended by the usually only rarely used functions, which are marked with a three-dimensional engraved effect.

The extended menu also opens by itself after a certain period without your having to click the arrow.

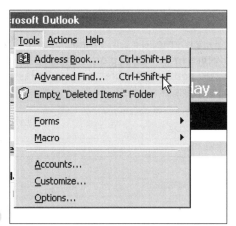

3 When you now use one of the extended menu items (here: ADVANCED FIND) Outlook 2000 memorises your choice and next time offers you this function...

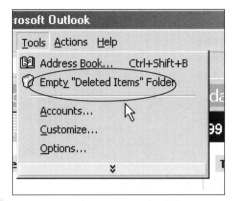

....as a normal component of the
menu. Thus the composition of the
menu bars is in a limited way depend-
ent on the behaviour of the user.

Let's briefly go through the individual menu options, starting with
the FILE menu.

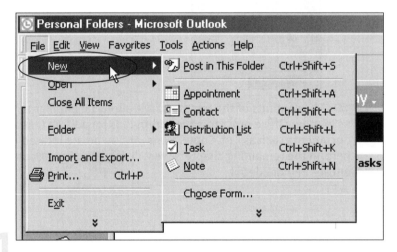

Via the FILE **menu** you can access all commands which are in
the broadest sense connected with file operations: opening and
closing files, saving, printing, importing, exporting, and so on.
Probably, the most important entry is NEW, with which you can
create **new entries** in Outlook.

**Importing**: Loading data from a different program in Outlook.

**Exporting**: Saving Outlook data in the format of a different program (for example Excel).

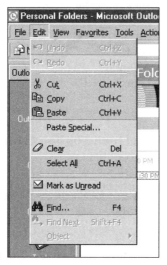

2 The contents of the EDIT **menu** will surely be familiar to you: as in other Office programs the commands for editing text and documents such as Cut, Copy, Delete, and so on are located here. In the remaining chapters we will describe the various entries in more detail.

**3** Under **VIEW** you will find everything which is related to the overall
appearance of Outlook. This
is where you determine how you
want Outlook to display your data.
For example in the VIEW menu of the
calendar, you can specify the number
of days which are shown together
in the calendar. Via VIEW you also
determine whether and with which
toolbars you want to work in Excel.

**4** The **FAVORITES menu** is new to Outlook 2000. However, it is not so much a
function of Outlook, as a system extension of Windows 98, which is looking
ahead to Windows 2000. Using FAVORITES IN OUTLOOK, you can access the functions of Internet Explorer and, therefore, Internet and Intranet data.
The FAVORITES menu does not only exist in Outlook but also – among other
places – in the START menu and in Windows Explorer and Internet Explorer.
With it you can work across different programs. However, it can also lead to
considerable confusion if you are not careful. The final section of Chapter 11 is
devoted to a discussion of the sense and nonsense underlying the concept of
FAVORITES.

**43**

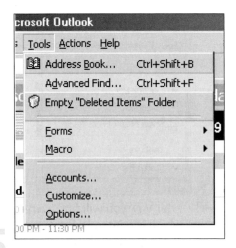

5 Under the Tools **menu** you can find all the entries which the developers of Outlook could not quite place elsewhere. Here are located some general functions, such as the FIND menu. However, the most important entries are ACCOUNTS, via which you create and manage your e-mail accounts, and OPTIONS, via which (together with CUSTOMIZE) you set central configuration options for Outlook and individual folders.

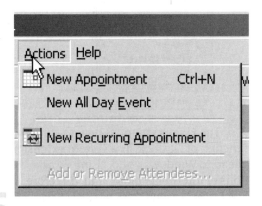

6 Under ACTIONS you can find a list of all the things you can do in the currently active folder. In this folder (calendar) this would be entering appointments or planning meetings.

**7** Finally, via the HELP menu you can access the various **help files** and **explanation functions** of Outlook.

# The toolbar

The operation of a program with as many options as Outlook 2000 exclusively via the menu is possible, but now and then very impractical. Consequently, there are so-called toolbars on which you can find small symbols that function as **shortcuts**. Instead of scrolling

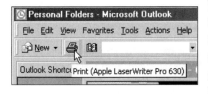

through menus and submenus, you simply click the appropriate symbol and thus call up the corresponding command. You can find out which symbol represents which command by pointing the mouse to the symbol:

a small window containing a brief description of the function appears. In many cases, however, this description is written next to the symbol.

Just like the menu bar, you can also place the toolbar wherever you want.

**1** Move the mouse pointer to the left margin of the toolbar.

**2** Again the mouse pointer turns into a four-sided arrow.

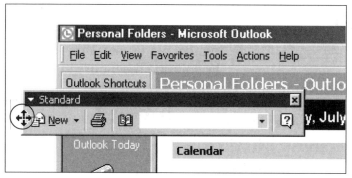

**3** Holding down the left mouse button, drag the toolbar into the appropriate position.

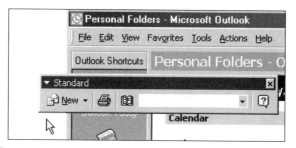

Release the mouse button. Done.

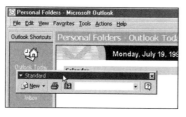

Just like for the menu bar, double clicking the top margin moves the toolbar back to where it came from.

In contrast to the menu bar with its unchanging structure, the toolbar almost always changes completely and displays different symbols.

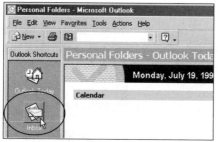

For example, when you switch from 'Outlook Today' to 'Inbox' (click once on the appropriate symbol) ...

**47**

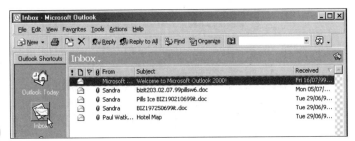

...the toolbar adapts to the new context and is equipped with typical e-mail commands such as *Reply* or *Forward*.

As the toolbars vary in size, it may happen that some of the symbols do not fit onto the toolbar. In this case there is displayed at the right edge of the bar a combination of a double and a downward pointing arrow. The double arrow indicates that there are more symbols, and the downward pointing arrow means that you can open a menu here.

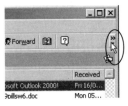

To find out what other symbols are on the toolbar, simply click the arrow combination.

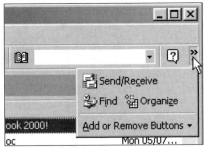

A menu with further symbols opens, from which you can choose the required command. As the button *Add/remove buttons* indicates, you can customise the toolbars according to your own preferences.

Only four symbols can be found on all toolbars, namely NEW, PRINT, FIND CONTACT, and HELP. It does not matter what you are currently doing; these four functions are always useful. Let's have a brief look at each of them in turn.

To the left on the toolbar you can always find the NEW symbol of the currently active folder. Here 'Outlook Today' is active, therefore you can open a new e-mail form by clicking the symbol (not the arrow!).

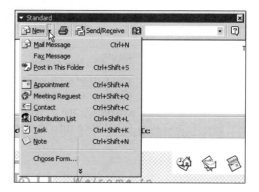

When you click the downwards pointing arrow next to NEW the complete NEW menu opens which you normally activate via the menu bar with FILE/NEW.

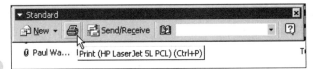

By clicking the printer symbol you can print out the currently active data record of Outlook. This may be an address, a memo, an e-mail message – in short, everything you manage and process in Outlook. The printing process starts immediately without any further prompts. The printout is carried out on the printer which is activated in the Windows control panel. You can find out which printer is activated by resting the cursor for a few seconds on the symbol (without pressing a mouse button) and reading the displayed help text.

Via the small entry box on the toolbar you can search your contact folder for particular entries, no matter where you currently are or what you are currently doing. Click once into the empty entry box...

...type in the name you are looking for, and click on the address book symbol. Alternatively you can simply press the ⏎ key. This function has been added to Outlook for the first time (in earlier versions it was a little more complicated to find specific addresses). It is so useful that one wonders why the programmers have not thought of it earlier.

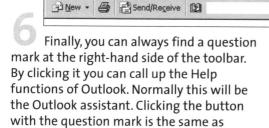

**6** Finally, you can always find a question mark at the right-hand side of the toolbar. By clicking it you can call up the Help functions of Outlook. Normally this will be the Outlook assistant. Clicking the button with the question mark is the same as pressing the [F1] key.

# The Outlook bar

The Outlook bar, with which the **navigation** within the Outlook data is facilitated, is located on the left-hand margin. In its basic function the bar is similar to the Windows Explorer, (which in Windows 2000 is supposed to look like the Outlook bar).

Just as you can access programs, folders, and files in the Explorer, you can access the various Outlook folders and data via the Outlook bar. The Outlook bar, however, contains symbolic links, whereas you can access files in the Explorer directly.

On the Outlook bar the icons – from 'Outlook Today' to 'Notes' – for the central Outlook folders are located by default. The individual icons are placed in different groups. By default the three groups are:

'Outlook Shortcuts' followed by...

...the groups 'My Shortcuts' and 'Other Shortcuts'. Each of these groups may contain any number of icons.

**1** You can easily switch between the groups. Simply click on the name of the respective group...

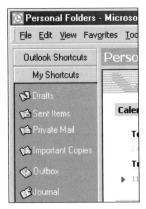

**2** ...and it will open with a pretty sliding-drawer effect.

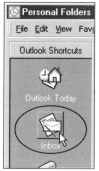

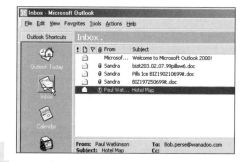

**3** When you click an icon...

**4** ... the required folder opens in the main window of Outlook.

You can also open folders in a **separate window** outside Outlook. Proceed as follows:

**5** Right-click the symbol of the relevant folder. In this way the context menu of the folder is called up.

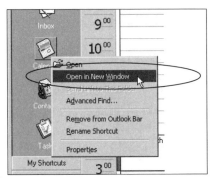

**6** Select the Open
in New Window entry..

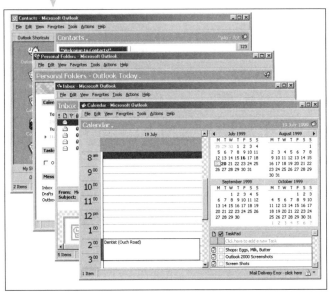

**7** In this way you can not only open two or more Outlook folders at the same time, but these folders are also independent of Outlook and thus can be moved freely across the screen, and remain open even if you exit Outlook 2000. In this example the following folders are open (from back to front): Outlook 2000 with the 'Contacts' folder, 'Outlook Today', the 'Inbox', and lastly the 'Calendar'. Each window is an independent unit of Outlook 2000.

# The status bar

The status bar is located at the bottom of the Outlook screen. As the name implies, you can find information about the current state (status) of Outlook or the active folder here. The status bar may not seem to be very useful at the beginning. However, you will notice that you use it more and more, for example, to gain information about how many elements a selected folder contains or how advanced the e-mail reception is, as the size of your Outlook database increases.

No matter whether you activate your appointment list, task list, or address list, the

19 e-mails, 7 unread

status bar always displays the **current number of respective elements**. In this example: The inbox (not shown) contains 19 e-mails of which 7 are unread.

As Outlook automatically executes certain processes, the program displays the respective operations on the status bar. In this example your **e-mail account** is regularly checked for new mail. To do so, Outlook automatically establishes a connection to your mail server (if you go online via a modem, Outlook automatically initiates the

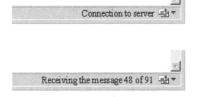

dial-up program to establish a connection to your Internet provider)...

...collects the new mail...

...and then terminates the connection to the mail server, that is, it hangs up.

## 3

# What's in this chapter:

Although Outlook 2000 is a very flexible and versatile program which offers you a multitude of options to organise your work with, its basic idea and general structure are relatively simple: the program manages entries into forms, which are stored in folders. This chapter will tell you how Outlook manages data, explain what an Outlook entry is, and outline what you can do with the program.

## You already know about:

## You are going to learn about:

# What is an Outlook entry ?

To you there are major differences between an appointment, a note, and an address. However, to Outlook 2000 there are no differences between these items. To the program every scrap of information is an entry. Each ENTRY consists of various **data fields** (for example a contact entry consists of name, address, phone number, and so on). The entries are recorded on **forms**, which are filed in folders.

You can regard Outlook as a cabinet full of ring binders. Different data are systematically recorded on forms that are neatly filed in the ring binders. In contrast to real ring binders, in which you can collect different documents, Outlook only ever files a specific type of form in a certain type of folder. The Contacts folder contains only Contacts forms, the Inbox only e-mails, and the Notes folder only notes, and so on.

Whether an entry is counted as an appointment or an address depends on two things only: in which folder and on which form the entry has been recorded.

Example: If you connect the name 'John Smith' with a date and a time, the entry becomes an **appointment**. If you connect it with an address and a phone number, it becomes a **contact**. Finally, if you link it with a start and end date, it is a **task**.

This may sound a bit abstract at the moment, but in practice it has real, and advantageous effects. As Outlook only distinguishes entries by the varying combinations of their attributes no matter in which folder they are located, it is very easy to change the properties of an entry.

Thus, you can quickly change a **note** into an **e-mail**, the e-mail into a **task**, and finally into an **appointment**. Thus, a hurriedly scribbled note in the end becomes a finished task, project, and so on.

Each entry may have a variety of data fields. A very simple entry in the **address book** may contain (if I have not miscounted) approximately 130 pieces of information. That is much much more than you probably are ever going to need.

TIP

I cannot repeat this often enough: Do not be intimidated by the extensive Outlook forms! You do not need to fill in all the data fields. Always remember: Outlook is there to help you, not the other way around.

This has advantages and disadvantages. The vast number of fields and their combinations make Outlook a very flexible tool for the management of all kinds of information.

On the other hand, an entry form usually looks more complicated than it actually is. Furthermore, to manage all the data and links the program requires a powerful computer.

However, one advantage is that almost all the processes in Outlook are very similar: once you have grasped how to enter an appointment, the managing of tasks will not pose any major problems for you.

In the following sections we will have a closer look at the general structures and options.

# Creating entries

Outlook is a program in which a variety of ways may lead to the same goal. This also applies to the creation of entries.

First, there is the official way via the menu bar:

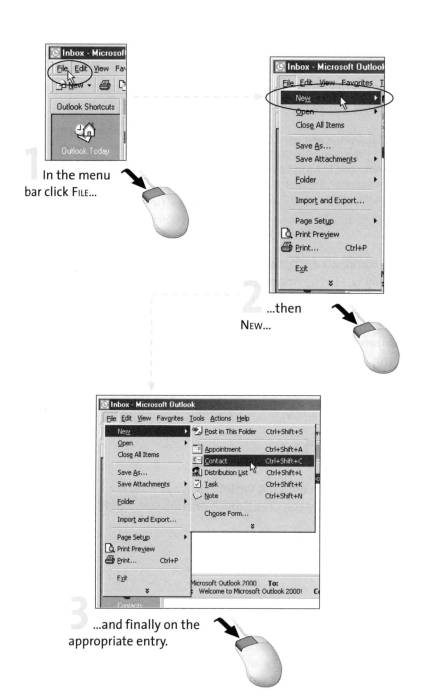

In the menu bar click FILE...

...then NEW...

...and finally on the appropriate entry.

If the toolbars are activated you can use this shorter way.

Clicking once on the symbol to the very left (not on the arrow!) creates a new entry in the currently active folder. For example, if you are in the calendar, you create new appointment entry, in the task list a new task, and s on. In this example the inbox is active, and thus clicking NEW opens a new e-mail form.

However, if you click on the arrow...

. ...the complete menu for creating new entries opens. In th way you can enter a new address from your inbox without having to switch to the contacts folder.

**61**

The third way is again via the Menu bar.

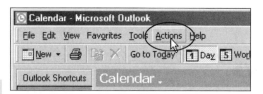

**1** Finally, there is the
ACTIONS menu option,
via which you...

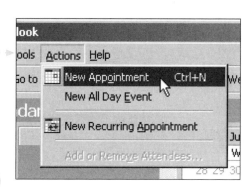

**2** ...can also create new entries. However, as by
clicking on the NEW symbol, you can only create new
entries for the currently active folder in this way. In
this example the calendar is active and you can only
create new appointments.

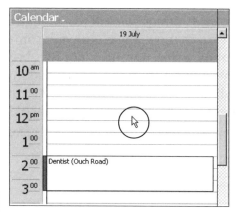

However, if you think that these three options are all you have, you are mistaken. You can also right-click an empty space in the currently active folder...

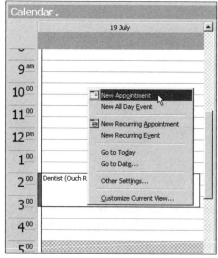

...and select the appropriate NEW entry from the context menu.

But that is not all: You can do without the right-click and instead simply double-click in the empty space of the folder. A form for new entries opens.

**63**

However, at Microsoft things sometimes happen as if you were on a shopping television channel: there is always something more to come. You do not have one, not three, not five, but six options to create a new entry! Apart from the mouse and the menu you can also use the keyboard. Via fixed keyboard shortcuts you can also create new entries. The most important shortcut keys are:

| Entry | Keyboard shortcuts (simultaneously press the following keys) |
|---|---|
| Appointment | Ctrl + ⇧ + A |
| Contact | Ctrl + ⇧ + C |
| Task | Ctrl + ⇧ + T |
| Note | Ctrl + ⇧ + N |
| E-mail | Ctrl + ⇧ + M |

These keyboard shortcuts always work, no matter where you currently are in Outlook. In this way you can, for example, create a new task without leaving your mail folder.

> **TIP**
>
> The initial letter of the respective term has been used as abbreviation in the keyboard shortcut:
>
> A = Appointment     C = Contact
> T = Task            M = Mail

# Changing entries

Addresses, appointments or task are not usually entered and saved permanently, but are continually changed. An appointment is postponed and the date has to be changed, an address has a different phone number now, or a friend has moved and thus you have to alter the address, and so on. In Outlook it has to be possible to change entries at any time – and of course it is.

For each entry there is a form, in which all data for this specific entry is managed. To change an entry, you only have to call up the relevant form, make the changes, and save the changed form.

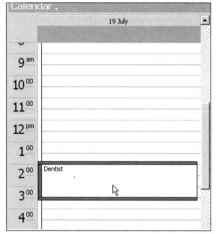

1 There are (of course) many ways to open the form. The easiest is to point to the entry and open it by double-clicking.

Alternatively by double clicking the entry, you can choose it with a single mouse click and open it by pressing the ⏎ key.

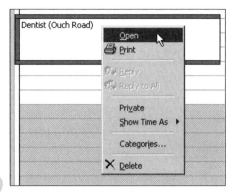

2 Or you can call up the context menu with the right mouse button, and then choose the item Open.

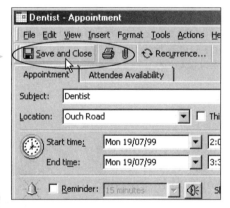

3 No matter which way you choose (there is at least one more option), the form of the entry, in which you can change or add details, opens. When you click *Save and Close*, Outlook saves the changes.

# Deleting entries

Admittedly it is very tempting to keep everything you have ever entered in Outlook, but it is not recommended. In this case Outlook would not only be burdened with the management of obsolete notes (which does not improve the speed of the program), but an unchecked collection mania would soon result in a pile of confusing data rubbish. And that is exactly what you are trying to avoid with Outlook.

**TIP** The entries are not really deleted, but are moved to the folder 'Deleted Items', from which you can restore them again.

Entries you do not need any more, old notes, finished tasks, and so on can of course be deleted. Naturally there are various ways to do this, too.

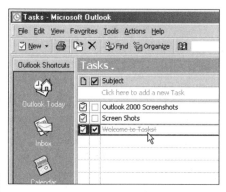

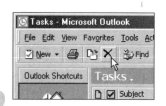

1 Mark the entry you want to delete by left-clicking it once.

2 Then **either** click the X on the toolbar...

**3** ...or simultane-
ously press the keys
⟨Ctrl⟩+⟨D⟩ ...

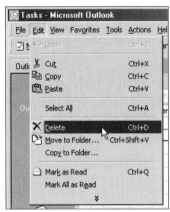

**4** ...choose the
menu option EDIT/
DELETE.

**5** You can also point to the entry you
want to delete – without activating it – with
the mouse...

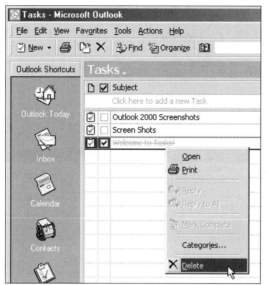

6 ...open the context menu of the active entry by right clicking it, and then choose DELETE.

Finally, it is also often possible to use the [Del] key. However in that case it may happen, you will not delete the marked entry, but delete the text of the entry.

# Marking several entries

If you want to look at several addresses, or delete several notes at once, or display several appointments side by side, you can either select or open each entry separately, or mark several entries and open (or delete) them with a single command.

There are two ways, in which you can mark **several entries at once**. If you want to mark neighbouring entries you can mark them as a block.

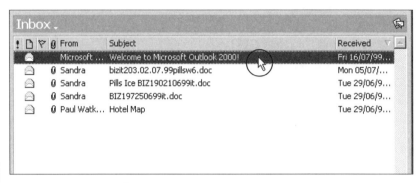

Left-click the beginning of the block you want to mark.

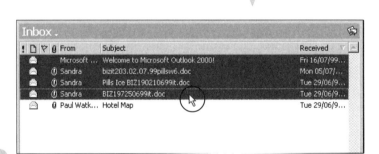

Hold down the ⬆ key, and click the final entry. The area between the first and the last entry has been marked. Now release the ⬆ key.

However, sometimes the appropriate entries are not located next to each other, but are distributed across a list. In this case you have to mark the entries one after the other.

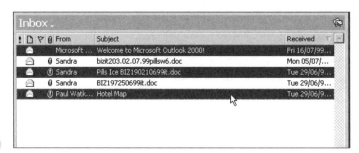

**3** Holding down the Ctrl key, mark the entries. In this way you join the entries into a group. When you click an already marked entry, while holding down the Ctrl key, the marking is removed again.

# Creating new folders

**Copying** from A to B: The entry exists in A as well as in B.

**Moving** from A to B: The entry is deleted in A and inserted into B.

If you always file your notes in a single folder, it will eventually burst at the seams and it will be impossible to find anything in the jumble. There is only one remedy for this: you have to divide the heap of notes into smaller portions and file them in separate folders.

You can and should do this in Outlook, too. Admittedly an Outlook folder can store any amount of information. However, it does not make for a particularly clear structure if you simply file all mail, whether private or business-related, important or less important, in the same folder.

However, before you can move or copy entries into a new folder, you have to create it first. Here is how you do it:

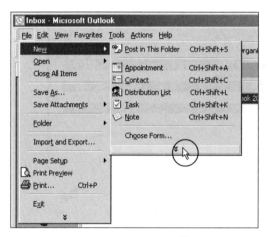

Choose FILE/NEW and open the extended menu by double-clicking the double arrow.

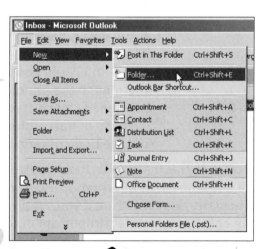

From the extended menu choose the item FOLDER.

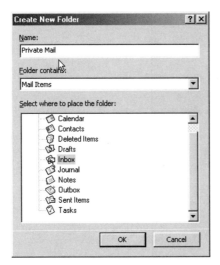

A new menu opens which provides access to the usually hidden folder structure of Outlook. First enter the name of the folder you want to create (in the example: 'Private Mail').

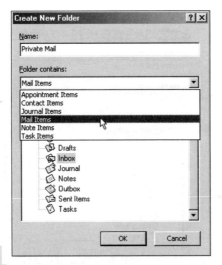

Then specify the folder type. In this case e-mail. (Remember: Each folder in Outlook can only manage one specific type of information.)

73

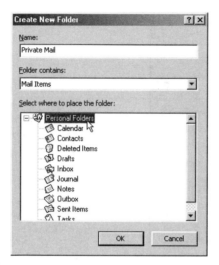

**5** Finally, determine where you want to create the folder. You can embed folders as much as you like, that is, create any number of subfolders in a folder. However, to start off with we had better remain on the highest folder level. Thus, select 'Personal Folders'.

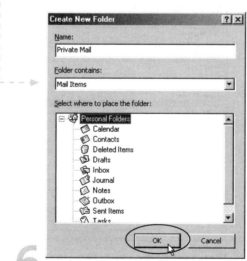

**6** The folder is created as soon as you click *OK*.

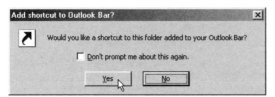

**7** To ensure problem-free access to the newly created folder, you should create a symbolic link on the Outlook bar. Outlook does this for you and asks you whether you wish to have such a link. Click on *Yes*.

**8** To indicate that the link has been created, 'My Shortcuts' on the Outlook bar flashes. When you open the bar with a mouse click, you can see the new symbol.

**9** You can now access the newly created folder in the same way as all other Outlook folders. When you click on the symbol...

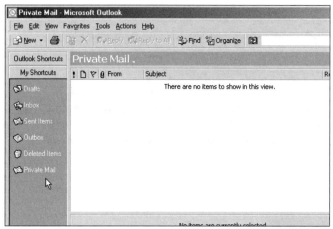

**10** ...the new empty folder for your private mail opens.

# Moving and copying entries

After you have created the new folder, you can move or copy Outlook entries to it. To move entries from the inbox to the newly created folder 'Private Mail', you have to proceed as follows:

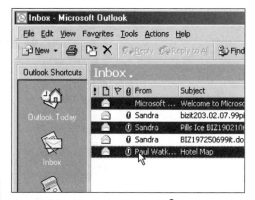

**1** Mark the entry (or entries) you want to move.

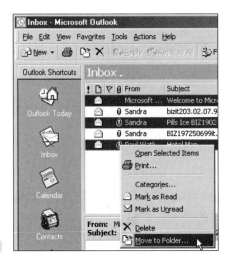

2 Call up the context menu via the right mouse button. The functions listed here are available for the marked entry. As the entries are to be moved into a different folder, that is exactly what you are going to choose, namely MOVE TO FOLDER.

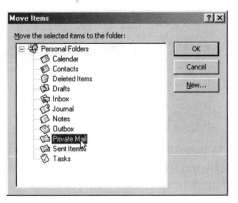

If you click the button NEW here, you will get into the dialog box in which you can create new folders.

3 A window opens from which you can choose a target folder (here: 'Private Mail').

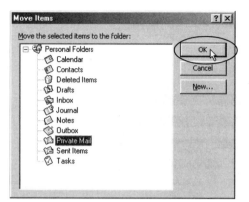

When you confirm your choice by clicking on *OK*, Outlook moves the marked entries from the 'Inbox' to 'Private Mail'.

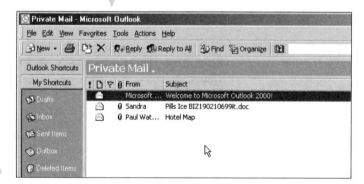

To check if everything has worked, we take a look at the new folder – and there it is: the previously empty folder now contains the four marked entries from the inbox.

It is just as simple to copy entries. However, copying takes slightly longer:

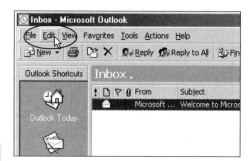

1 Mark the entry you want to copy, and select the EDIT option from the menu bar.

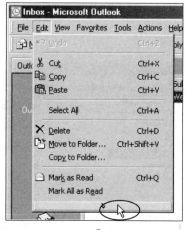

2 Open the extended menu by double-clicking the double arrow, and...

...select COPY TO
FOLDER.

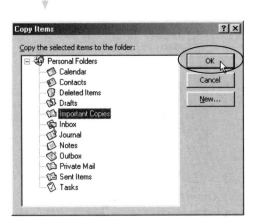

Again a window opens from which you can select
the target folder – in this example the previously newly
created folder 'Important Copies'. Confirm with *OK*. The
entry is then copied. It now exists in the original folder
'Inbox' and in the folder 'Important Copies'.

# Moving entries between different folders

So far you have only moved or copied entries between folders of the same type, that is from one e-mail folder to another e-mail folder.

This usually makes sense, but you can also move or copy entries between folders of different types. However, this also changes the type of the entry.

Outlook compares the entry that is to be moved with the structure of the target folder and then creates an appropriate new entry. It is rather as if you could make an instant appointment by simply re-filing an address entry.

What exactly happens during copying depends on what type of entry you want to copy and to where.

A simple example will illustrate the principle: You want a quickly scribbled shopping list to become a task, to ensure that you will definitely not forget to do your shopping. Subsequently an overview of the most important combinations will be given.

Shops: Eggs, Milk, Butter

19/07/99 12:10 PM

**1** First open the folder from which you want to copy an element. In this example click the 'Notes' icon on the Outlook bar.

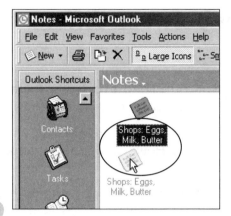

**2** Left-click on the entry you want to copy, and holding down the mouse button...

**3** ... drag the cursor onto the symbol of the appropriate folder (here: 'Tasks'). Then release the mouse button.

When dragging & dropping an entry in Outlook, you can see a shadow-like copy of the entry at the cursor. At the same time the cursor changes, and displays a small box at its lower end. Both symbols indicate that you are moving or copying entries.

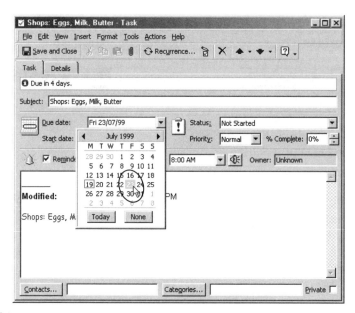

The task form opens. The contents of the note
are now in the text box of the task. You can now enter
a date on which you want to do your shopping.

Leave the form by clicking
on *Save and Close*.

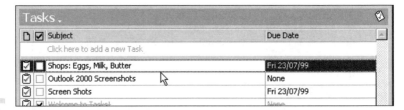

**6** The contents of the note have been added to your task list.

It is not sensible to copy any type of entry to other folders. What exactly happens is outlined in the following overview.

| Entry type | Copy to | Effect |
|---|---|---|
| E-mail | Outlook Today | **CAUTION!** The message is moved to an area, which is only accessible via the full text search! This is probably an error in Outlook 2000. |
| | Contacts | The sender of the e-mail message is entered into the address book; the complete text of the e-mail is inserted into the annotations box. |
| | Calendar | An appointment with the 'Subject' of the e-mail as title and the mail message as annotation is created. |
| | Tasks | A task with the 'Subject' of the e-mail as title and the mail message as annotation is created. |
| | Notes | The complete e-mail is inserted into a new note sheet and the cursor is placed above the mail text for annotations. |
| Contacts | Outlook Today; inbox | A new mail message to the e-mail address of the contact is created. |
| | Calendar | A meeting request is sent to the e-mail address of the contact. |
| | Tasks | A task request is sent to the e-mail address of the contact. |
| | Notes | The contact information is copied to a new note sheet. |
| Tasks | Outlook Today; inbox | The contents of the task are inserted as text into a new e-mail form. |
| | Calendar | An appointment with the task as annotation is created |
| | Notes | The complete task text is inserted into a new note sheet and the cursor is placed above the text for annotations. |
| Notes | Outlook Today; Inbox; Contacts; Calendar; Tasks | A new, empty form is opened in each case and the contents of the note are copied to the annotations box of the new form. Thus, it is very easy to create a task or an appointment from a note. |

## 4

**The task list**

## What's in this chapter:

Plain but effective: the task list in Outlook is a powerful tool. Here you can quickly and without difficulty write down what you have to do. But that is not all: even complicated scheduled project planning is possible with the task list. This chapter teaches you how to create tasks, assign due dates to tasks, and set the automatic task reminder.

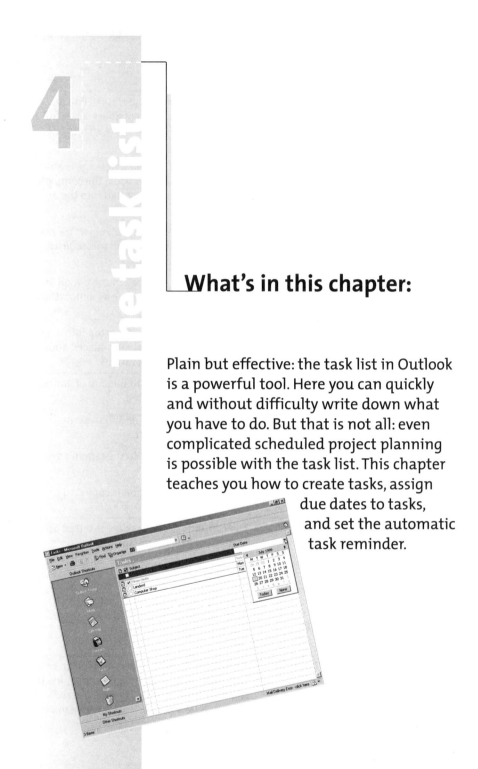

## You already know about:

## You are going to learn about:

# Creating tasks

Doing the shopping, taking the car to the garage, writing your final report, calling a colleague, booking cinema tickets, and so forth: there are many things we have to do every day. Some are of a private nature, others are business-related; some are important, others are less so; there are tasks which have a set date, and others for which there is no particular schedule. Most tasks are one-off jobs, some recur at regular intervals. Without notes and task lists you very easily lose the overall view.

But not with Outlook: to cater for the multitude of occasions, task management in Outlook is versatile and flexible. You can create tasks in various ways – from a quick note every now and again, and precise schedule planning, to the regularly occurring task.

If you quickly want to insert an entry into the task list, proceed as follows:

You can also access the task list from the calendar.

If the task list is not active, click once on the task symbol and open the corresponding folder.

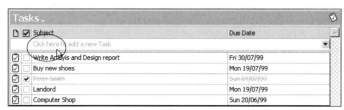

**2** Click in the empty text box at the top of the task list.

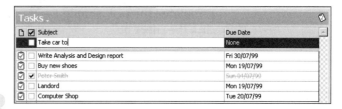

**3** The mouse pointer turns into the cursor symbol, and you can enter your task.

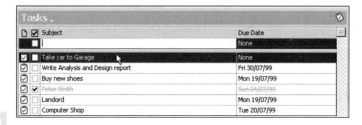

**4** When you have finished making your entry, press the ⏎ key. Outlook adds the task to the task list.

**89**

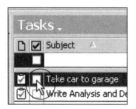

5 As soon as you have completed the task, simply click the check box.

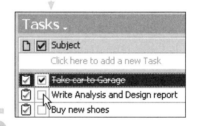

6 The task is ticked as completed and crossed out.

# Assigning due dates to tasks

Often, a task has to be completed by a specific date. In these cases you simply mark the entry in the task list with the due date. Outlook then ensures that you do not miss your deadline.

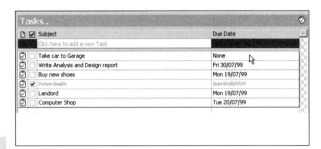

Click once in the appropriate box of the 'Due Date' column, in which the 'None' entry is inserted as default..

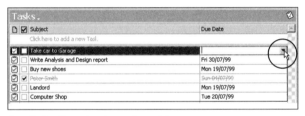

The default entry is replaced by an empty field box and a small arrow appears at the right-hand margin. Click the arrow.

A calendar sheet opens. Simply click the appropriate date.

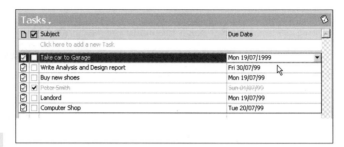

**4** The calendar disappears again, and a due date has been assigned to the task.

Of course it is no problem to assign due dates via the calendar. However, if you want to enter 'tomorrow' or 'next Tuesday' without knowing the exact date, there is an easier way.

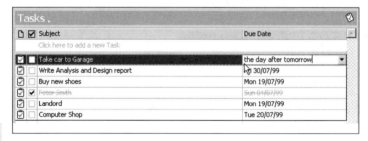

**1** Instead of opening the calendar, simply enter the explanatory text.

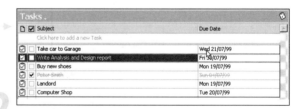

**2** Outlook then calculates the date automatically.

**Caution!** Don't assume that Outlook is infallible. The date entry only works if the 'Due Date' box was previously empty ('None'). If it wasn't previously empty, Outlook will make a hash of the date. Also, don't make it too complicated. 'The day after tomorrow' will work, but 'The day after the day after tomorrow' will simply come out as 'The day after tomorrow'.

# The task form

Sometimes a simple note and a due date are not enough to record a task fully. In these cases the complete task form has to be used.

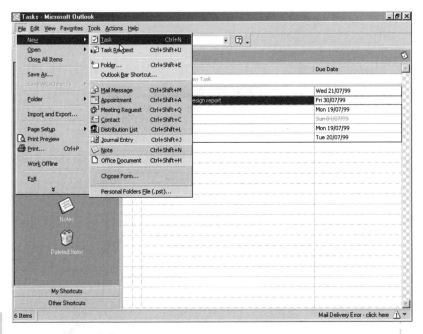

Open a new task form by choosing the TASK option from the NEW menu or by pressing the keyboard shortcut Ctrl + ⇧ + T

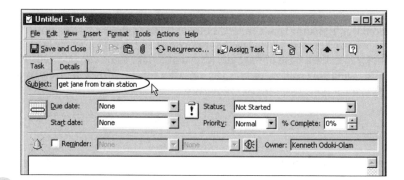

 On the form specify the subject first. Simply click in the corresponding text box, and enter the text.

 Via the calendar you also specify the due date on the form without a linguistic specification like 'Tomorrow'.

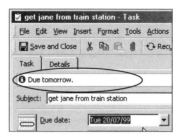

4 After you have entered the date Outlook displays an information bar, which tells you how much time you have scheduled for the completion of the task.

5 In contrast to working with the task list, here you can additionally specify a start date for the task. Enter the date following the usual procedure.

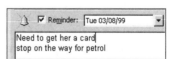

6 You can enter any text – for example an address, a phone number, or any other useful remarks relating to the task – in the big annotations window.

**95**

Sometimes a task requires you to phone, visit, or otherwise contact a person. In these cases you can link a task to an address from the contacts folder. To link a task and a contact proceed as follows:

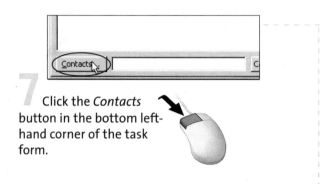

**7** Click the *Contacts* button in the bottom left-hand corner of the task form.

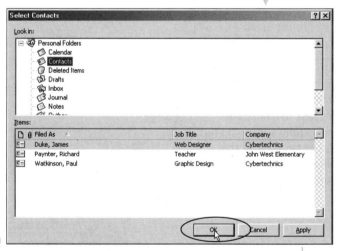

**8** A window opens. Mark the appropriate name and confirm with *OK*. The name is added to your task form.

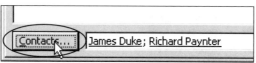

**9** If you want to link several names to a task, repeat these steps as often as required.

When the task becomes due, you can now easily and quickly access the required contact data.

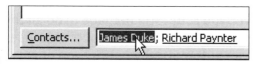

**10** Simply double-click the name.

**11** The corresponding form of the contacts folder opens.

**97**

**12** As with all other Outlook 2000 forms, the task form is closed by clicking the *Save and Close* button. One more entry has been added to your task list.

# Setting the automatic task reminder

So far, so good! However, you could still manage to do all this with a task list and a normal pocket diary. Outlook 2000, of course, can do more. For example, it can automatically remind you of any recorded task, so that you won't forget it.

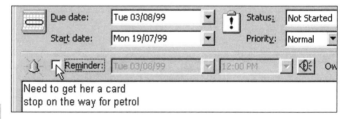

**1** On the task form activate the *Reminder* check box. The previously dimmed, grey, and thus inactive areas become active entry boxes.

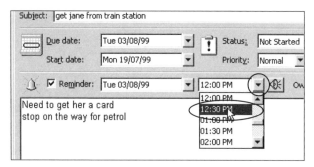

2 In these boxes you can specify the date and time you want to be reminded to complete the task. As usual you can open the menu to specify the time by clicking the downward pointing arrow next to the time.

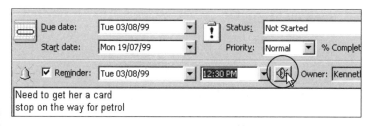

3 Furthermore, you can specify a melody, which Outlook will play as an acoustic signal. Click the speaker symbol...

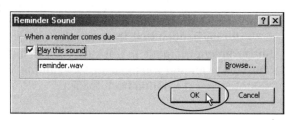

4 ...and choose the appropriate sound file. Confirm your choice with *OK*.

**99**

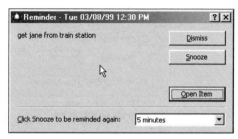

**5** As soon as the reminder is due, a message will be displayed on your screen, and Outlook will play the specified sound.

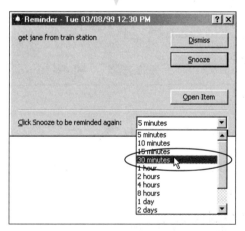

**6** It may happen that the reminder is given at an inconvenient moment. In this case you can instruct Outlook to remind you again in, for example, 30 minutes. Select a period from the list...

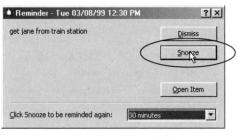

7 ...and close the reminder
window by clicking on *Snooze*.

# Creating recurring tasks

There are tasks that occur at regular intervals, for example, creating a
back-up copy of your most important data. With Outlook you can
also easily record tasks of this type.

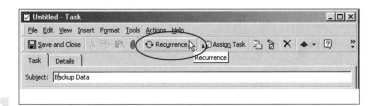

1 On the toolbar of the task form
click the *Recurrence* button.

101

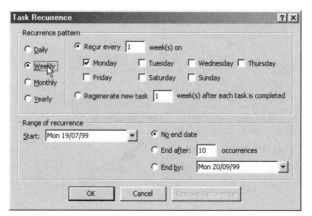

2 An entry form opens, in which you can specify in detail,
the interval you want the task to be recorded in your task
list.

3 First
determine the
interval: is the
task due daily,
weekly, monthly,
or even yearly?

4 Then you can specify the exact
pattern of the recurrence. The
options are adapted to the
respective interval (days, weeks, and
years).

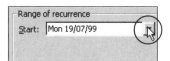

**5** Then enter the start date of the recurring task. Open the already familiar calendar by clicking the downward pointing arrow. Choose a date.

**6** If the recurrence of the task has a time limit (for example a holiday coverage), this is where you can specify the date by which it will end.

**7** Finally, confirm your entry with *OK* and thus enter the recurring task into your Outlook task list.

With a bit of practice you can create almost any type of interval you can think of. The following are a few examples:

**103**

A task has to be carried out **every two days**. The corresponding entry will look like this:

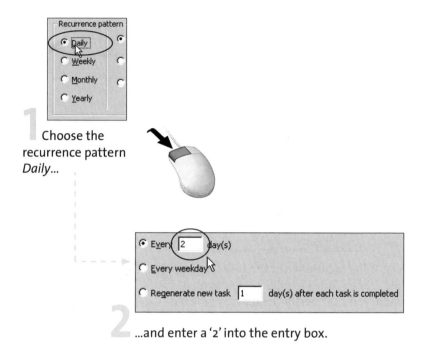

**1** Choose the recurrence pattern *Daily*...

**2** ...and enter a '2' into the entry box.

The entry for a task that recurs every **two weeks** on **Wednesday** and **Friday** looks as follows:

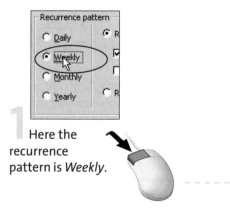

**1** Here the recurrence pattern is *Weekly*.

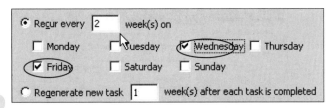

Then enter a '2', and activate *Wednesday* and *Friday* by clicking in the box in front of the days.

**Every first Thursday of the quarter** (that is every three months)

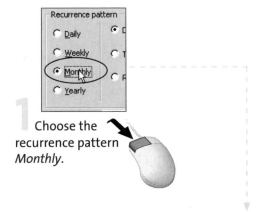

Choose the recurrence pattern *Monthly*.

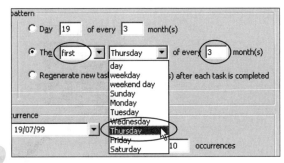

Then set the counter to the appropriate interval.

**105**

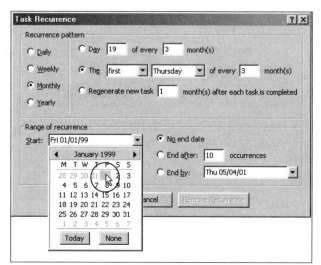

**3** To ensure that your calculation of the quarter corresponds to the calendar year, select the first day of the current quarter (that is the 1 January, 1 April, 1 July, or 1 October) as the start date.

Finally an example of a yearly recurring task. Let's say the **second Wednesday in April.** Proceed as follows:

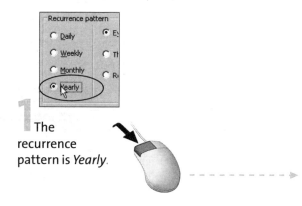

**1** The recurrence pattern is *Yearly*.

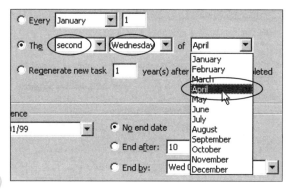

The exact interval is again specified with the help of the various drop-down lists.

# Options and settings

In the task list, overdue tasks are usually marked in red, and completed tasks in light grey. The time scale of the reminder function starts at 8 a.m. If you do not like this simply change it.

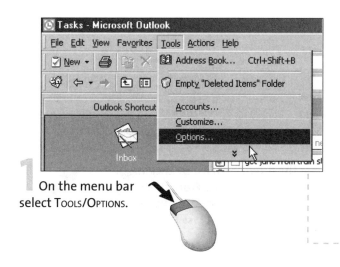

On the menu bar select TOOLS/OPTIONS.

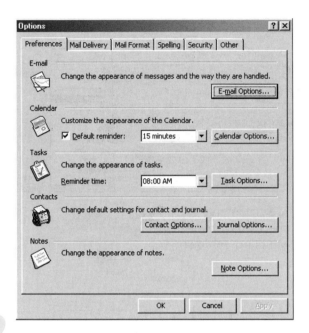

The *Options* dialog box opens. In it you can configure Outlook 2000 via clearly structured tabs. At the moment, however, we are only interested in the *Tasks* item on the *Settings* tab.

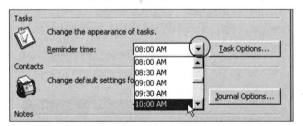

Open the drop-down list by clicking the downward pointing arrow. From this you can choose the default time at which you want Outlook to remind you of tasks that are due.

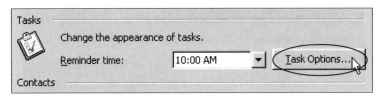

**4** By clicking the *Task Color Options* button ...

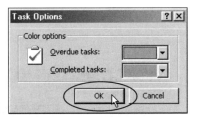

**5** ...you can specify the colours of the task display. Make your choice and close the dialog box using *OK*.

Furthermore, you also have the possibility of customising the reminder option. These settings are quite difficult to access. The Outlook programmers (probably rightly) assumed that users hardly ever want to change these default settings. However, if you want to do it, this is how to proceed:

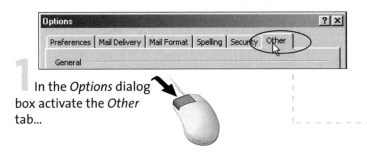

**1** In the *Options* dialog box activate the *Other* tab...

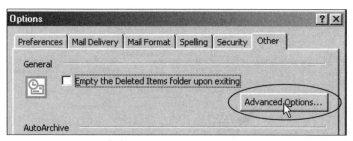

...then click the
*Advanced Options*
button...

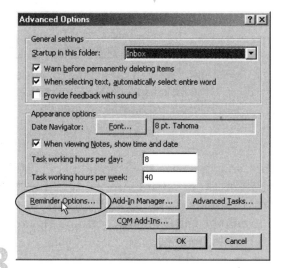

...and then on
*Reminder Options.*

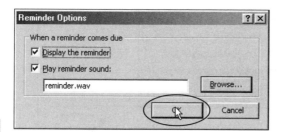

**4** A dialog box opens in which you can specify whether you want to be reminded with a message or with a sound file. By clicking on *Browse* you can search your hard disk for suitable sound files. Usually the default setting will be enough. Close the dialog box using *OK*.

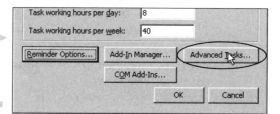

**5** In this way you can return to the *Advanced Options* menu. Using the *Advanced Tasks* button, you can open a further menu...

**111**

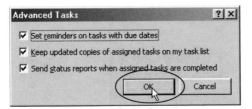

**Advanced Tasks**  ? X

☑ Set reminders on tasks with due dates

☑ Keep updated copies of assigned tasks on my task list

☑ Send status reports when assigned tasks are completed

OK    Cancel

**6** ...in which you can specify details of the reminder option. Here too we recommend not changing the default settings to start with. Again leave the dialog box by clicking *OK*.

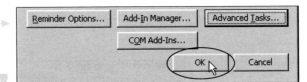

Reminder Options...   Add-In Manager...   Advanced Tasks...

COM Add-Ins...

OK    Cancel

**7** You return to the *Advanced Tasks* menu, which you also leave using *OK*.

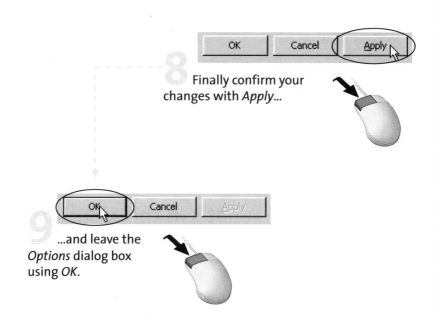

**8** Finally confirm your changes with *Apply*...

**9** ...and leave the *Options* dialog box using *OK*.

# What's in this chapter:

Omnipresent and inevitable: appointments, appointments, appointments. This chapter teaches you how to manage your appointments with Outlook. This does not automatically guarantee that you will have your appointments under control. You probably also won't become a shining example of punctuality over-night. However, the program will make a big difference. The appointment form has already been introduced in the first chapter. Here we will mainly introduce the intensive use of the mouse. You can create almost all entries in the calendar by simple clicking and dragging.

**You already know about:**

**You are going to learn about:**

# The calendar screen

As a calendar on its own, it is not particularly helpful; it is displayed by default together with the task list in Outlook.

**1** Open the calendar with a single click on the calendar symbol on the Outlook bar.

**2** The default display offers you an overview of the appointments of the currently active day and a monthly calendar overview in the top right-hand corner. The task list is displayed in the bottom right-hand corner.

| July 1999 | | | | | | | August 1999 | | | | | | |
|---|---|---|---|---|---|---|---|---|---|---|---|---|---|
| M | T | W | T | F | S | S | M | T | W | T | F | S | S |
| 28 | 29 | 30 | 1 | 2 | 3 | 4 | | | | | | | 1 |
| 5 | 6 | 7 | 8 | 9 | 10 | 11 | 2 | 3 | 4 | 5 | 6 | 7 | 8 |
| 12 | 13 | 14 | 15 | **16** | 17 | 18 | 9 | 10 | 11 | 12 | 13 | 14 | 15 |
| 19 | 20 | 21 | 22 | 23 | 24 | 25 | 16 | 17 | 18 | 19 | 20 | 21 | 22 |
| 26 | 27 | 28 | 29 | 30 | 31 | | 23 | 24 | 25 | 26 | 27 | 28 | 29 |
| | | | | | | | 30 | 31 | | | | | |

| September 1999 | | | | | | | October 1999 | | | | | | |
|---|---|---|---|---|---|---|---|---|---|---|---|---|---|
| M | T | W | T | F | S | S | M | T | W | T | F | S | S |
| | | 1 | 2 | 3 | 4 | 5 | | | | | 1 | 2 | 3 |
| 6 | 7 | 8 | 9 | 10 | 11 | 12 | 4 | 5 | 6 | 7 | 8 | 9 | 10 |
| 13 | 14 | 15 | 16 | 17 | 18 | 19 | 11 | 12 | 13 | 14 | 15 | 16 | 17 |
| 20 | 21 | 22 | 23 | 24 | 25 | 26 | 18 | 19 | 20 | 21 | 22 | 23 | 24 |
| 27 | 28 | 29 | 30 | | | | 25 | 26 | 27 | 28 | 29 | 30 | 31 |
| | | | | | | | 1 | 2 | 3 | 4 | 5 | 6 | 7 |

3 In the monthly overview you can scroll backward and forward with the small arrows on the right and left respectively.

4 Choose the calendar sheet you want displayed by simply clicking the appropriate date.

The highlights in the monthly overview have the following meanings:
Red border = Current date
Grey background = Date currently displayed as a calendar sheet
Bold = For this day there is at least one recorded appointment

**117**

The number of months displayed in the overview is infinitely variable. Simply reduce or enlarge the display with the mouse. Proceed as follows:

Move the mouse pointer to the bottom margin of the calendar overview. As soon as the mouse pointer changes...

...drag the frame, while holding down the mouse button. The number of the displayed months is adjusted automatically.

**3** Of course, you can do this on the left margin, too. Holding down the left mouse button...

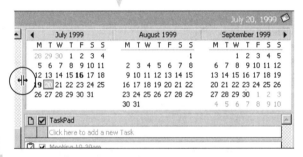

**4** ...drag the frame. With this procedure you can arrange any number of months in any way you want. The total width of the monthly overview determines the total width of the task pad.

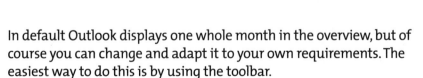

In default Outlook displays one whole month in the overview, but of course you can change and adapt it to your own requirements. The easiest way to do this is by using the toolbar.

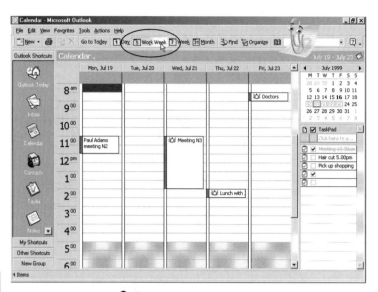

1 *Work Week* displays the current week from Monday to Friday.

2 The *Weekly View* displays the calendar week from Monday to Sunday without a time schedule as in a pocket diary.

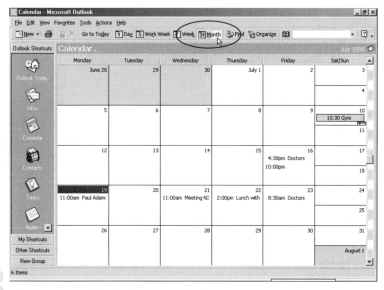

3 The view *Monthly* displays a complete month. However, in this view you have to do without the monthly overview and the task pad.

In the monthly view it may happen that there is not enough space. In this case a small button will represent an appointment which is not displayed.

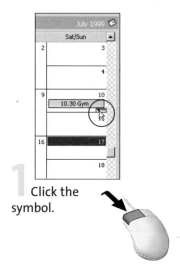

1 Click the symbol.

**121**

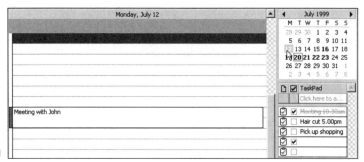

2 The daily view of the corresponding appointment opens.

But this is not all: you can also display any number of days. These days do not have to be in sequence.

1 To display a series of days which cannot be displayed using the display options available to you – for example Monday to Thursday – proceed as follows: click the first day of the period you want Outlook to display. Hold down the left mouse button, and simultaneously press the ⇧ up key.

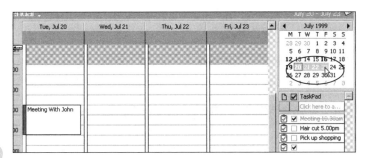

2 Then drag the mouse pointer up to the appropriate date. Outlook displays the selected days next to each other in the calendar (in this example: 17 to 20 May).

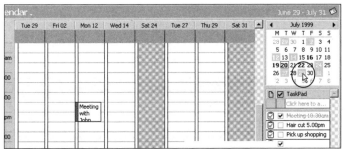

3 To mark a collection of days which are not in sequence, click each date while pressing the [Ctrl] key.

# Setting the calendar as the start screen

Outlook starts with the default 'Outlook Today' folder. Initially this is quite useful, but once you have a bit of experience you will probably want to see your calendar immediately after start-up. After all 'Outlook Today' only provides a general overview, whereas the calendar permits full access to all your appointments and tasks. Fortunately the developers of Outlook have remembered to provide an option to change the start-up properties of Outlook.

The method is admittedly a bit long-winded, but quite simple nevertheless. This is how you do it:

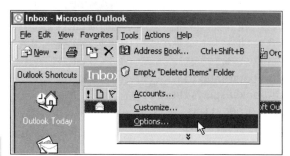

**1** Open the Options dialog box by choosing the OPTIONS entry from the TOOLS menu.

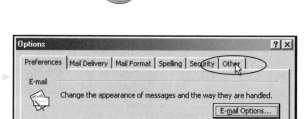

**2** Do not stay here, but quickly switch to the Other tab ...

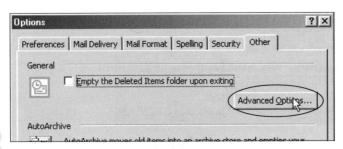

...and from here to the Advanced Options dialog box.

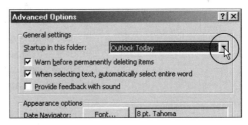

By clicking on the arrow under Startup in this folder, you can open a drop-down list...

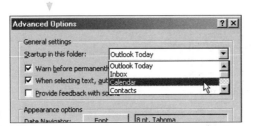

...in which you can specify 'Calendar' as the start-up folder (apart from the calendar you can also instruct Outlook to display any of the other folders at start-up).

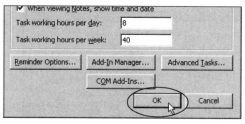

**6** When you close the dialog box by clicking OK, you return to the Options dialog box.

**7** Close this dialog box by clicking OK. Done! In future, Outlook 2000 will automatically display your calendar after start-up.

# Entering appointments

The main function of the calendar is the management of your appointments. The easiest and quickest way to enter an appointment is by typing it directly into the calendar sheet without using the appointment form.

**1** If the appropriate day is not active, simply choose it from the monthly overview.

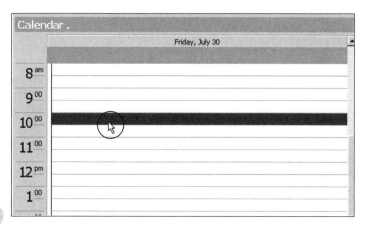

Click once in the row with the start time of the appointment. The row is now highlighted in blue.

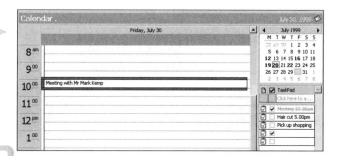

As soon as you start typing, the row turns into a field box with the usual flashing cursor. Now enter your appointment.

For your appointments as well as for your tasks the most important thing is efficiency and not style or beauty. You do not have to spell everything perfectly or be witty. It is enough that you can understand what you have written.

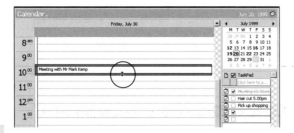

**4** Determine the appointment's end date by moving the cursor onto the lower edge of the entry until it turns into a double arrow.

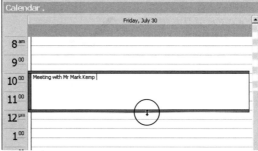

**5** Now you can enlarge the appointment window according to taste, until the appointment has been entered correctly.

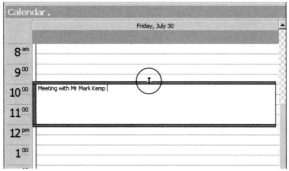

**6** You can proceed in the same way if you want to change the beginning of the appointment. Move the cursor to the upper edge of the appointment window, until it turns into a double arrow.

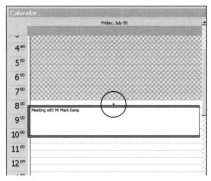

**7** Drag the edge of the window.

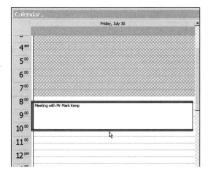

**8** As soon as you have completed the entry according to your requirements, confirm it by pressing the ⏎ key. Outlook has recorded your appointment.

Sometimes it may happen that two appointments have to be entered at the same time: for example, if it can only be possible to decide later on which appointment you actually want to keep, or if you are expecting an important call during a planned conference. Some electronic appointment planners assume that you cannot be in two places at the same time and thus do not permit the entry of two parallel appointments. Fortunately Outlook is not as fussy and restrictive.

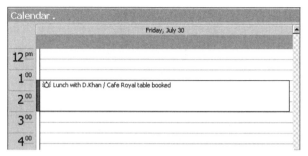

1 When creating a second appointment proceed in the same way as for the first: on the time bar click the start time for the second appointment.

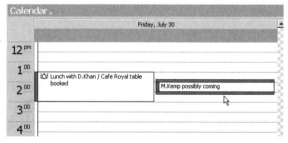

2 On the right-hand margin of the calendar sheet you can see that Outlook has highlighted the respective row in blue (as it does for creating a single appointment, too).

3 Without any further ado, you can now begin to enter your appointment. As soon as you start typing, Outlook displays two parallel appointment entries.

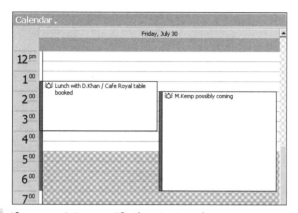

4    If appropriate, specify the start and end time of your second entry using the mouse, and finally record it in the calendar by pressing the ⏎ key. Done.

We all know that not only are there appointments that take one or two hours, but also appointments which take up the whole day. In Outlook these types of appointment are called 'events'. You can create events in the following way:

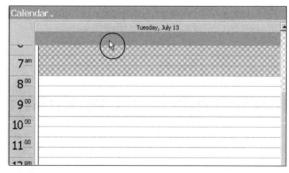

1    Click the grey area between the date and the start of the timetable of the calendar sheet.

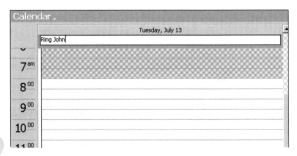

The dark grey box turns into a white field box. Now you can simply start to type, just as you can for appointment entries.

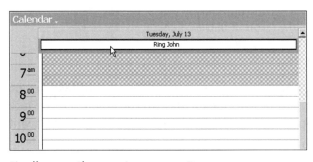

Finally, save the event by pressing the ⏎ key.

# Moving or copying appointments

Again and again it will happen that appointments are rescheduled. In a paper-based appointments book you have to cross out the old entry and add a new one. If several appointments are rescheduled in a week or a month the calendar pages soon look a mess and it is difficult to make out which appointments are still on and which are not.

Moving appointments in Outlook is not only easy, but it also does not leave any traces.

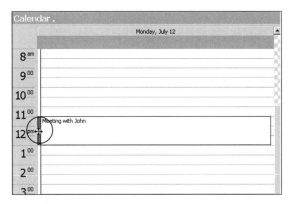

1 Move the cursor to the left-hand edge of the entry, until it turns into a four-sided arrow.

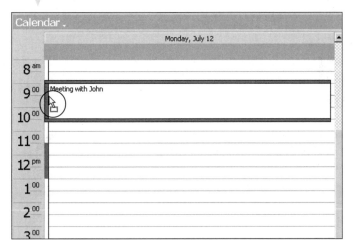

2 Then, holding down the left mouse button, drag the entry to where you want it. Release the mouse button. The appointment has (literally) been moved.

In the same way you can not only change the time but also the date of an appointment.

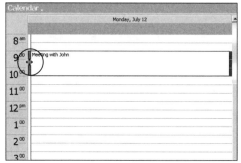

1 Move the mouse pointer to the left-hand edge of the appointment you want to move, until it turns into a four-sided arrow.

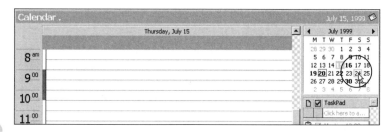

2 Holding down the left mouse button, in the monthly overview move the entry to the new date.

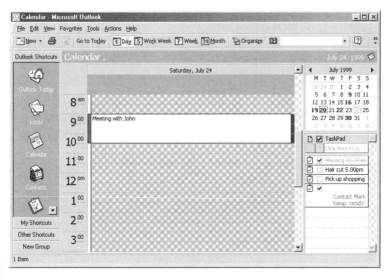

Now release the mouse button. Outlook then moves the entry to the new date and switches to the corresponding calendar sheet.

Instead of moving appointments, it is sometimes necessary to copy them. This procedure is just as simple as moving appointments. In addition you have to press the (Ctrl) key. To copy an appointment from one day to the next, proceed as follows:

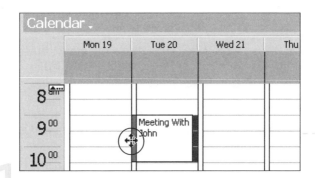

Move the mouse pointer to the left edge of the entry, until it turns into a four-sided arrow.

**135**

Holding down the ⟨Ctrl⟩ key, simultaneously press the mouse button, and drag the entry to where you want it. The small plus sign indicates that the marked entry is copied and not moved.

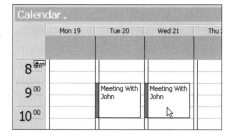

When you release the mouse button and the ⟨Ctrl⟩ key, the entry is copied to the chosen place.

However, Outlook would not be Outlook if there was not a different way to copy or move appointment entries.

| Calendar ⌄ | | | |
|---|---|---|---|
| Mon 19 | Tue 20 | Wed 21 | Thu |

8

9⁰⁰  Meeting With John

10⁰⁰

First turn the mouse button into a four-sided arrow by pointing it to the left-hand edge of the entry box as before.

| Calendar ⌄ | | | |
|---|---|---|---|
| Mon 19 | Tue 20 | Wed 21 | Thu |

8

9⁰⁰

10⁰⁰  Meeting With John

Nothing new so far – but this time hold down the right button, while dragging the entry to the appropriate place.

| Calendar ⌄ | | | |
|---|---|---|---|
| Mon 19 | Tue 20 | Wed 21 | Thu |

8

9⁰⁰  Meeting With John

10⁰⁰  Move

11⁰⁰  Copy

Cancel

When you release the mouse button, a small menu opens in which you can choose (with the left mouse button as usual) whether you want to copy or move the appointment to the marked place, or whether you prefer to cancel the whole operation.

**137**

# Combining the task list and the calendar

In the calendar view, tasks and appointments are displayed together not only for reasons of clarity, but also because you can easily create an appointment from a task, or assign a task to an appointment. It frequently happens that a task is created from a phone call that has been recorded in your calendar, or that the completion of a task requires a phone call.

And this is how you do it:

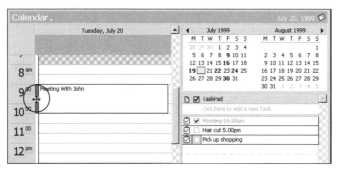

**1** Move the mouse pointer to the left-hand edge of the appointment to which you want to assign a task.

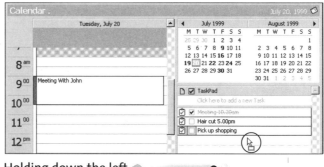

**2** Holding down the left mouse button, drag the entry into the task pad.

The appointment is **neither** deleted **nor** moved by the operation but is left in its original condition.

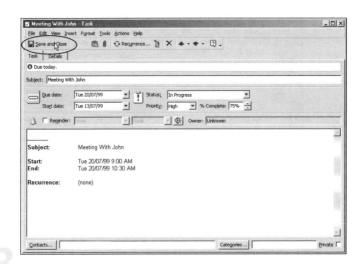

**3** Now release the mouse button. Outlook opens a task form, in which the appointment data has already been entered. You can enter additional data and then insert the form into your task list by clicking Save and Close as usual.

Of course you can add an appointment to a task by carrying out the reverse operation.

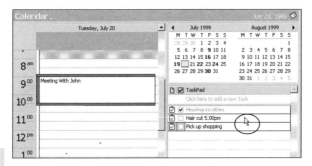

**1** Move the cursor onto the entry in the task list to which you want to assign the appointment.

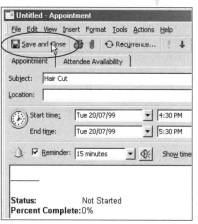

**2** Holding down the left mouse button, drag the entry into the calendar.

**3** Release the mouse button. Outlook then opens an appointment form in which the task data has already been entered. Fill in the rest of the form. You have to at least enter the time, as Outlook always enters 00:00 as the start and end time. Then add the entry to your calendar by clicking on Save and Close.

# The appointment form

In the last section you encountered the appointment form, which we are now going to deal with in more detail. The form is very similar to the task form. It also offers many more **appointment management** options than the methods outlined so far.

Admittedly, the extensive forms make the recording and management of appointments more flexible, but also a lot less transparent. The appointment form is quite intimidating with its many field boxes, drop-down lists, and buttons. However, always remember that you do not need to worry about that. The purpose of the program is to help you. Use those boxes you feel are useful, and simply ignore the rest.

As always in Outlook, many ways lead to the same goal. Correspondingly, there are many possibilities for opening a new appointment form. The easiest way is using the menu bar or the corresponding keyboard shortcut.

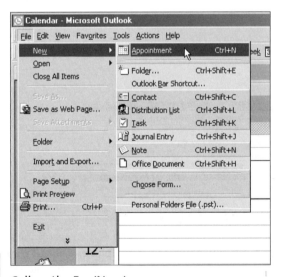

1 Call up the FILE/NEW/ APPOINTMENT menu option, or simultaneously press the [Ctrl]+[⇧]+[A] keys.

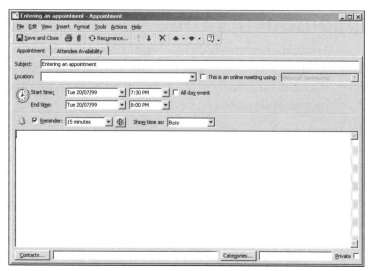

In the appointment form you can enter significantly more detailed information (including annotations of almost any length you want and cross-references to contact data) for the respective appointment than in the simple calendar view.

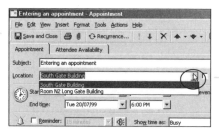

Apart from the subject, which is the reason for the appointment, you can also enter a place, where, for example, a meeting or a conference will be held. Simply type the place into the field box, or (after clicking on the downward pointing arrow) select a place from the drop-down list. In this list, all the place specifications you have ever used for appointments are saved.

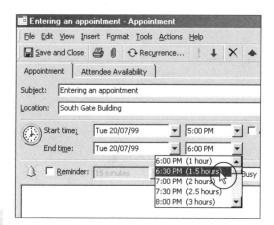

**4** You can specify the date and time with the mouse using the already familiar drop-down lists.

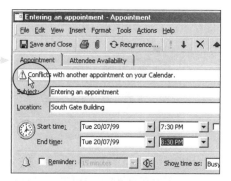

**5** If your current scheduling conflicts with an existing appointment, Outlook will dispatch a message to that effect. You can then either adjust the appointment accordingly or simply ignore the message. In any case you will be able to enter the appointment.

**143**

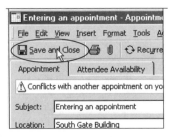

6 As usual the appointment is inserted into the calendar, when you click the Save and Close button.

# Planning appointments which last several days

Vacations and trade fairs have at least two things in common: both have to be planned and both last longer than one day. Of course in Outlook you can also manage appointments which last several days. You can only do this using the appointment form. However, the procedure is very easy.

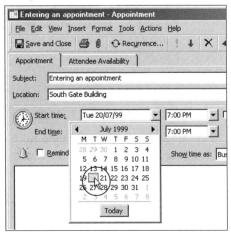

1 First determine the start of the appointment...

...then click
the All day event
box...

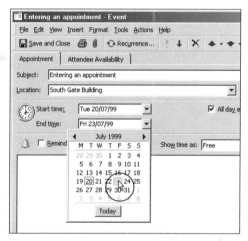

...and enter the end
of the event.

**145**

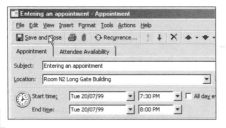

After you have saved and closed the appointment as usual...

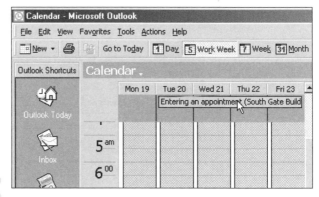

...Outlook displays the event in the top row of each calendar sheet.

# Planning recurring appointments

Birthdays and bank holidays are not the only examples for **recurring appointments**. Also lectures, tutorials, conferences, and meetings often take place at regular intervals. To make it possible to manage such appointments with Outlook, the **appointment form** offers the option to create recurring entries. (You have already worked with recurring entries in the task form.)

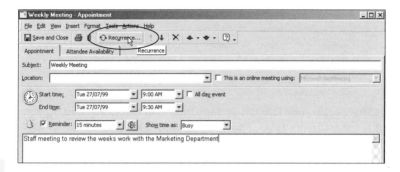

1  Fill in the appointment form as usual. However, instead of entering a date, click the Recurrence button.

2  Specify the start and end of your appointment here. Using the Duration drop-down list, Outlook can calculate the end of an appointment for you.

The 'Recurrence Pattern' is determined in the same way, as it is for recurring tasks. There is one snag: Outlook automatically inserts the current date. If on a Wednesday you want to enter an appointment, which takes place every Monday morning, you have to mark Monday and delete the tick in front of Wednesday.

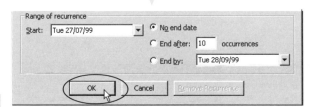

If appropriate, specify the start and the end of the series, and confirm the entry by clicking OK.

After you have inserted the appointment series in the calendar having clicked Save and Close...

**6** ...you can see that an appointment has been recorded for every Monday (in the monthly overview).

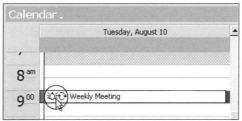

**7** In the calendar you can recognise a recurring appointment by a circular arrow symbol.

# Cancelling recurring appointments

Cancelling recurring appointments is as easy as creating them.

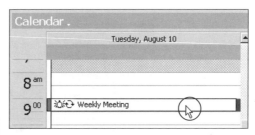

**1** Right-click any entry of the appointment series.

**149**

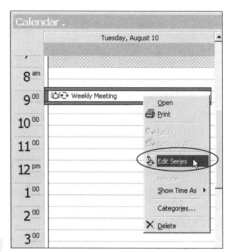

In the context menu which opens, choose the EDIT SERIES entry.

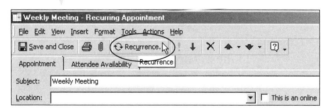

The appointment form of the current entry opens. Click the Recurrence button...

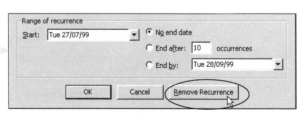

...and cancel the series with a mouse click.

# Options and settings

Some basic information such as your normal office hours, or the length of your working week has to be recorded to ensure that Outlook can manage your appointments correctly. Normally the default settings of Outlook will do, but if they do not, you can (of course) adjust them to your requirements. This is how you do it:

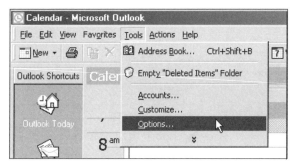

Open the Options dialog box, by calling up the TOOLS/ OPTIONS menu command.

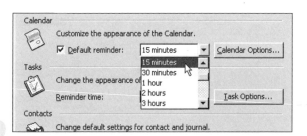

First, you can specify when you want Outlook to remind you of an appointment. The reminder for any appointment entered in Outlook is by default played 15 minutes before the appointment takes place. You can extend or reduce this period by almost as much as you like...

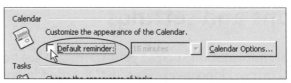

**3** ...or even switch it off completely. If you deactivate the default reminder, every new appointment is automatically recorded without a reminder. If necessary, you have to enter the reminder manually.

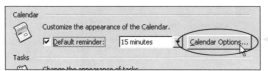

**4** Using the calendar options, you get to the core of the appointment functions.

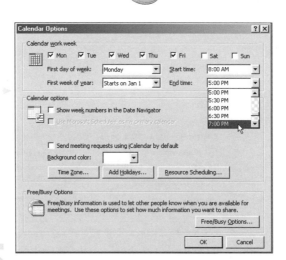

**5** Most of the options are only applicable to special cases and you should leave the default values unchanged. To you the 'Calendar Work Week' area is of interest. Here you can specify the days and office hours of your working week, and instruct Outlook how to determine the first week of a new year.

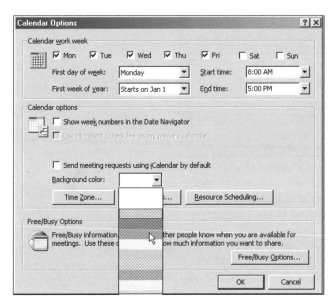

If you do not like the light yellow background of the calendar sheets, this is where you can choose a different colour.

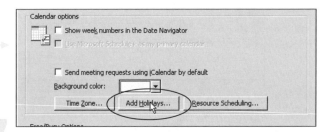

Via the button Add Holidays...

**8** ...you can open an extensive drop-down list, from which you can choose numerous national and religious holidays. The chosen holidays are then displayed in the calendar.

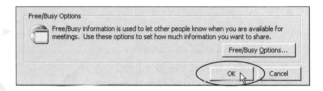

**9** Finally, close the dialog box with OK.

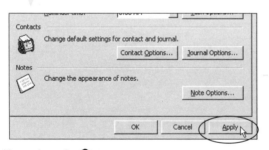

**10** You return to the Options dialog box. Click Apply and...

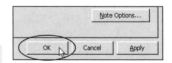

**11** ...close the dialog box via OK.

Finally, you can adjust the timetable into which Outlook divides the calendar sheets to your requirements. In default Outlook uses 30 minutes steps. You can change this as follows:

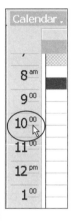

**1** Right-click in the time scale...

**2** ...and choose the appropriate scale from the context menu.

**3** Outlook applies the selected intervals.

# 6

## What's in this chapter?

Everything used to be so easy: your private and business friends had one address, one phone number, and one fax number. Today everything is different: a lot of people have a fax number, a second phone number, a mobile number, one or several e-mail addresses, a pager number, and so on. A simple note in your address book is not enough anymore. However, as an Outlook user you have everything under control, because the program manages a lot more than just a name and a few numbers. After all you are not only dealing with addresses but – as the name of the folder implies – with contacts.

## You already know about:

## You are going to learn about:

# Recording phone numbers

Outlook manages all addresses and phone numbers in the 'Contacts' folder. The choice of name already points to the fact that Outlook is far more than an ordinary address book. However, that should not keep you from using Outlook to jot down names and phone numbers quickly.

If the Contacts folder is not active, open it by clicking the corresponding symbol on the Outlook bar.

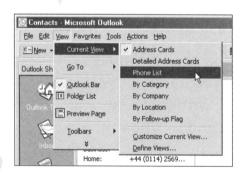

Change the address display (by default, Outlook shows you the address information in the form of small index cards) – if appropriate – by calling up the VIEW/CURRENT VIEW/PHONE LIST menu command.

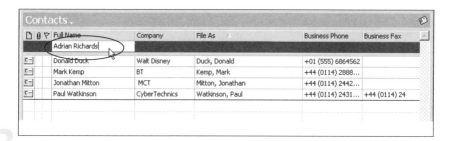

| | | | Full Name | Company | File As | Business Phone | Business Fax |
|---|---|---|---|---|---|---|---|
| | | | Adrian Richards | | | | |
| | | | Donald Duck | Walt Disney | Duck, Donald | +01 (555) 6864562 | |
| | | | Mark Kemp | BT | Kemp, Mark | +44 (0114) 2888... | |
| | | | Jonathan Mitton | MCT | Mitton, Jonathan | +44 (0114) 2442... | |
| | | | Paul Watkinson | CyberTechnics | Watkinson, Paul | +44 (0114) 2431... | +44 (0114) 24 |

**3** In the *Phone List* view, you can quickly enter the most important details of an address, such as the name and the phone numbers of your current caller. If you like, you can always add the remaining data later on. Click in the field under *Name*, and enter the name. You do not need to deal with the sequence of name and first name, Outlook will do that for you.

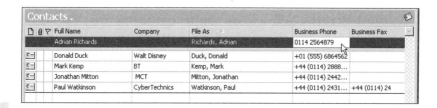

| | | | Full Name | Company | File As | Business Phone | Business Fax |
|---|---|---|---|---|---|---|---|
| | | | Adrian Richards | | Richards, Adrian | 0114 2564879 | |
| | | | Donald Duck | Walt Disney | Duck, Donald | +01 (555) 6864562 | |
| | | | Mark Kemp | BT | Kemp, Mark | +44 (0114) 2888... | |
| | | | Jonathan Mitton | MCT | Mitton, Jonathan | +44 (0114) 2442... | |
| | | | Paul Watkinson | CyberTechnics | Watkinson, Paul | +44 (0114) 2431... | +44 (0114) 24 |

**4** With the key you can get into the next field. Alternatively you can click on the field. One way or the other: as soon as you leave the name field, Outlook displays the typical sequence 'Name, First Name' in the Save as column.

**159**

| | | | Full Name | Company | File As | | Business Phone | Business Fax | |
|---|---|---|---|---|---|---|---|---|---|
| | | | Donald Duck | Walt Disney | Duck, Donald | | +01 (555) 6864562 | | |
| | | | Mark Kemp | BT | Kemp, Mark | | +44 (0114) 2888... | | |
| | | | Jonathan Mitton | MCT | Mitton, Jonathan | | +44 (0114) 2442... | | |
| | | | Adrian Richards | | Richards, Adrian | | 0114 2564879 | | |
| | | | Paul Watkinson | CyberTechnics | Watkinson, Paul | | +44 (0114) 2431... | +44 (0114) 24 | |

Contacts

**5** When you press the ⏎
key the entry is saved and
automatically added to your
address list. Done!

# Creating contacts

If you want to record more details than is possible in the list view,
you have to open – exactly as for appointments and tasks –
a corresponding **form.**

If you think that the task and appointment forms are complicated,
prepare yourself for a shock: the form with which Outlook manages
new addresses and phone numbers is far more complex. You can
assign more than 100 different entries and details to a contact. There
are 19 fields to record phone, mobile and fax numbers alone. For each
contact, three addresses plus three e-mail addresses can be entered.

As always in Outlook 2000, you should remember not to be
intimidated by the numerous options available in the form. Nobody
will force you to fill in all the fields. You cannot make a fool of
yourself. If only one name and a phone number are entered in the
huge form, both might look somewhat forlorn, but that does not
matter to Outlook at all. The purpose of the program is to manage
your data and nothing else. And this is what the software does,
without complaining or protesting, and no matter how much or
how little you enter. So, fill in the fields you need and ignore the rest.
Let's go.

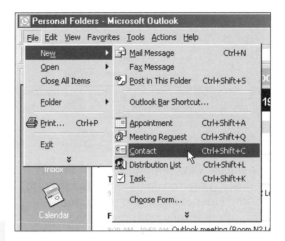

1 Open a new contact form using the FILE/NEW/CONTACT menu command. Alternatively you can press the Ctrl+⇧+C shortcut keys.

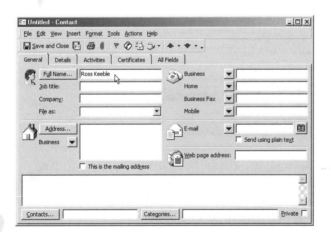

2 What you will see is an extensive form, but do not be intimidated by the many fields, tabs, and options. For now, we will ignore the various buttons and arrows. Click in the name field and enter the name.

**161**

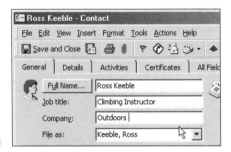

As in the list view, jump to the next field by pressing the ⇧ key. You do not have to take care of the sorting order of name and first name, as Outlook automatically takes on this job.

Normally Outlook saves the names in the common sequence of 'Name, First Name', but of course you can change that. Click the downward pointing arrow, and choose one of the listed sorting options.

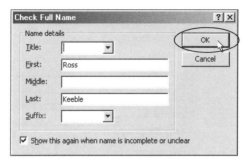

If Outlook finds a name problematic and cannot distinguish between family and first name, a small window opens in which you can give appropriate instructions to the program.

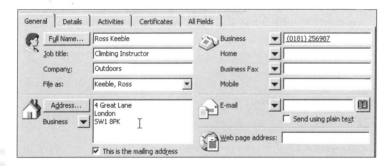

Fill in the remaining fields according to your requirements. With the key you can jump from one field to the next in the order of the fields. With the mouse button you can click any field you want and then enter data.

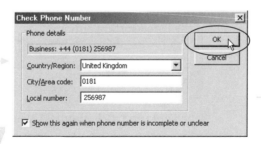

As for the recording of names, Outlook also attempts to correctly interpret phone numbers...

**163**

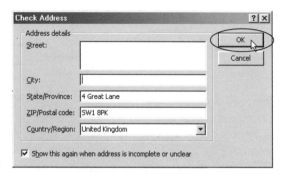

...and address entries. If this is not possible – for example because the postcode is missing – a corresponding dialog field opens, in which you can complete the phone number or the address. Incidentally: if you do not know a postcode – or other details – or do not wish to enter it, simply click *OK* and Outlook is content with what you have entered.

Finally, you can enter the e-mail address and, if available, a Web address. Nowadays, it is not only companies that have a page on the Web, but also more and more private individuals. Today, these two entry fields are almost as important as phone numbers.

When entering a Web address, you do not have to enter the character sequence 'http:/'. Outlook automatically adds it after you have left the field.

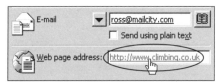

When you now move the mouse pointer onto the Web address, it turns into a pointing hand. Left clicking starts your Internet browser which automatically connects to that Web address.

**HTTP = Hypertext Transfer Protocol.** This abbreviation is an important technical piece of information that instructs an Internet browser about which method it has to load and display data from the Internet. Apart from HTTP there are other methods (so-called protocols). However, by now they have been substituted almost completely by HTTP. Thus, HTTP has become the default protocol, which is automatically selected by the browser if no other protocol has been specified.

You have now entered the entire address. However, Outlook would not be Outlook if it did not possess numerous additional options. And this is justified; after all there are always addresses and phone numbers that simply do not fit into a fixed default pattern.

Let's have a look at the various buttons of the contact form.

If you do not trust Outlook with the analysis of a name or want to enter a more unusual name, simply click the button Name.

**165**

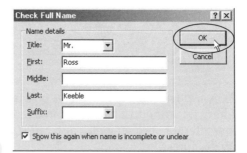

This opens the corresponding dialog box. After you have completed the entry close the dialog box using *OK*.

Similarly, you can treat address which do not fit the usual pattern. Click the *Addresses* button.

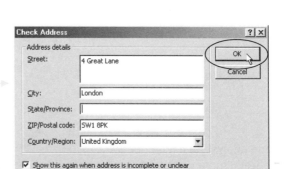

The corresponding dialog box opens. Leave the dialog box using *OK* after you have completed your entries.

5 The address book symbol next to the e-mail address has a different function. You do not open a dialog box to make entries with it, but...

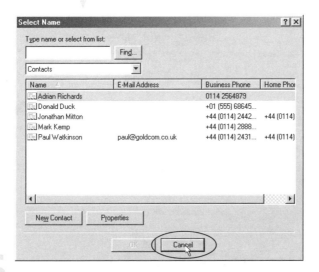

6 ...to open the Windows address book. This is an address list, which is independent of Outlook and – so to speak – the predecessor of the Contacts folder. Every name you record in the address book is also registered in the Contacts folder and vice versa. It could be said that the address book is superfluous as you now have Outlook, but under certain circumstances it can still be useful. However, in Windows the number and the disarray of the various address indices causes confusion for beginners. Simply ignore it and click *Cancel*.

**167**

As extensive as the form may be, you simply cannot fit all contact data you enter onto the screen. On the other hand: who really needs to be able to see all 19 phone numbers, three addresses, and three e-mail addresses at once? Consequently, the Outlook programmers have thought of something: instead of, for example, showing all phone numbers at once, you can choose four numbers from a list, which are then displayed. You can access the remaining numbers via a drop-down list.

By default, the four fields are reserved for entries for 'Business', 'Private', 'Business Fax', and the unavoidable 'Mobile'. You can change this in the following way:

Click the downward pointing arrow next to the field where you want to change the contents.

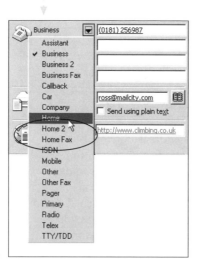

Choose the appropriate entry from the comprehensive drop-down list. A tick indicates that you have already assigned a phone number to the entry.

**3** The entry is substituted immediately. If the newly chosen entry is still empty...

**4** ...you can fill it in, and if you so choose...

**5** ... switch back to the original entry. By temporarily displaying the entries, you can record all the phone and fax numbers for the contact one by one.

**169**

In principle, this procedure also works for the various addresses and e-mail addresses, the only difference being that you have one out of three instead of 4 out of 19. Here follows a brief demonstration of the procedure for addresses:

1 Click the downward pointing arrow, and choose the required address.

2 Outlook changes from 'Business' to 'Private'.

If you now think that this is all the data you could ever enter into a contact form, you are mistaken. Have a look at the remaining tabs for each entry. However, these fields are only used – if at all –by advanced users of Outlook. Here again, the rule to ignore everything you do not understand still applies.

In the scope of this book and this chapter we will restrict ourselves to one further recommendation: at the bottom of the form you can find a field box and a *Contacts* button, with which you can link the active entry to other 'Contacts' entries. In this way you can easily link, the manufacturers of a product and its suppliers for example, or a company and its press agency, or simply a group of friends.

Oh – as always, you can finish working with a form by clicking *Save and Close*.

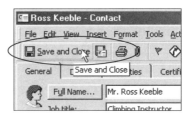

# Working with contacts

The recorded contacts are not only an address and phone list which you use when you want to phone a customer, colleague, or friend, but they also ease your everyday work.

Often, you are in contact with several members of a company. Their addresses only vary by name and by phone extension. Outlook saves you the effort of repetitive typing. You can avoid having to enter the same address and main phone number by proceeding as outlined below:

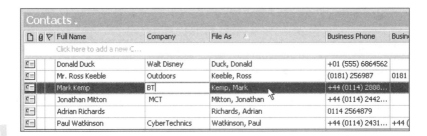

Choose an entry with the required company address.

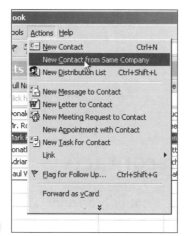

Call up the
OPERATIONS/NEW CONTACT
FROM THE SAME COMPANY
menu command.

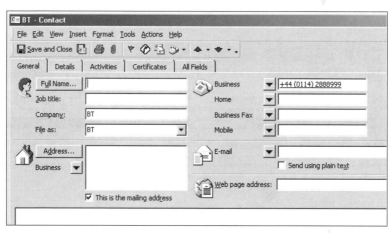

Outlook opens a new contact form and
automatically enters the company name and the
phone number of the existing entry.

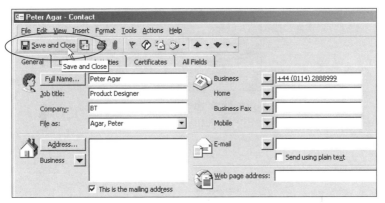

**4** Now you can enter the name of the member of staff and any other minor details. When you have completed your entries you can insert the entry...

| ☐ | 🔗 | ∇ | Full Name | Company | File As ▲ | Business Phone | Business Fax |
|---|---|---|---|---|---|---|---|
| | | | Click here to add a new C... | | | | |
| ☐ | | | Peter Agar | BT | Agar, Peter | +44 (0114) 2888... | |
| ☐ | | | Donald Duck | Walt Disney | Duck, Donald | +01 (555) 6864562 | |
| ☐ | | | Mr. Ross Keeble | Outdoors | Keeble, Ross | (0181) 256987 | 0181 256987 |
| ☐ | | | Mark Kemp | BT | Kemp, Mark | +44 (0114) 2888... | |
| ☐ | | | Jonathan Mitton | MCT | Mitton, Jonathan | +44 (0114) 2442... | |
| ☐ | | | Adrian Richards | | Richards, Adrian | 0114 2564879 | |
| ☐ | | | Paul Watkinson | CyberTechnics | Watkinson, Paul | +44 (0114) 2431... | +44 (0114) 24 |

**5** ...into the contact folder using the *Save and Close* button. Done!

It is even easier to send e-mail messages to contact addresses. The prerequisite for this is, of course, that you have configured Outlook for sending and receiving e-mail (how you do this is outlined in the next chapter).

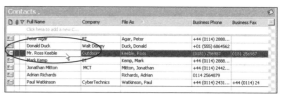

Right-click the entry to which
you want to send a mail message.

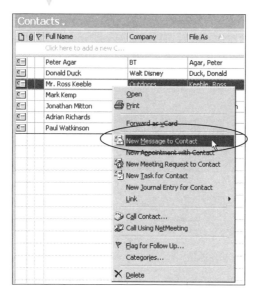

The context menu of the
entry opens. Choose NEW
MESSAGE TO CONTACT.

**3** Outlook opens a new mail form, inserts the e-mail address from the contact entry, and places the cursor in the *Subject* box. You can start typing at once.

Using the context menu you can – apart from sending e-mail messages – also...

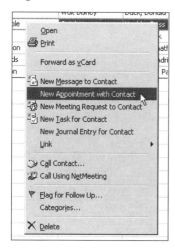

**1** ...create an appointment...

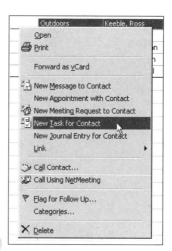

**2** ...or a task, which is connected to the currently active contact entry.

As a component of Office 2000 Outlook 2000 (of course) works in conjunction with the other Office programs. For example, Outlook is used by the other programs for sending documents via e-mail. You can also access Word from Outlook, and with a few mouse clicks insert an address into a letter in Word.

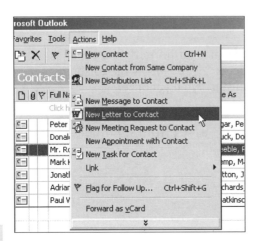

**1** Activate the appropriate contact entry. Then call up the OPERATIONS/NEW LETTER TO CONTACT menu command.

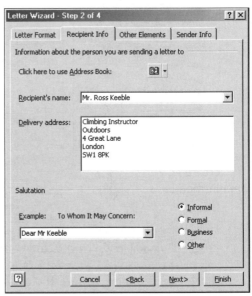

**2** Outlook then starts Word and hands over the necessary contact data to the letter wizard of Word.

# Options and settings

Compared to the calendar or the task list settings, there are rather fewer configuration options for the Contacts folder. They were probably only listed in the *Options* dialog box by the Outlook developers for reasons of completeness.

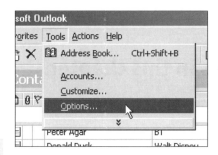

Open the *Options* dialog box by calling up the TOOLS/OPTIONS menu command.

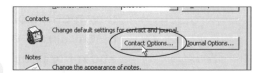

Clicking the *Contact Options* button takes you...

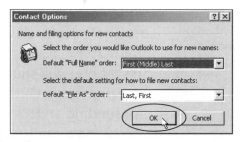

...to a dialog box in which you can modify the order in which Outlook saves and displays the contacts. Normally you do not need to change a lot here. If, nevertheless, you want to change something, make a choice by opening a drop-down list using the arrow buttons, and select the appropriate sorting type. By clicking the *OK* button you can close the dialog box again.

## What's in this chapter:

During the last few years electronic mail – e-mail for short – has established itself, slowly but surely, as probably the most important new method of communication. It is an essential part of everyday office life and more and more people also use e-mail privately as an ideal addition to the telephone. Therefore it is not surprising that Outlook possesses a powerful and versatile e-mail module. For reasons of clarity we are going to deal with this topic in two chapters. This first chapter will show you how to prepare Outlook for sending and receiving e-mail.

## You already know about:

## You are going to learn about:

# Setting up an e-mail account

TIP

You have to have an Internet or network connection to be able to use e-mail.

Before you can send or receive e-mail with Outlook, you have to prepare the program to use e-mail: without a so-called 'e-mail account' you cannot go ahead.

An e-mail account is used for the management of your name and e-mail address. Outlook can manage several e-mail accounts. This is useful and makes sense, if you have several e-mail addresses, for example a business and a private e-mail address.

Outlook prompts you to create such an account when it first starts up. However, you can create an e-mail account at any time.

In the course of the account installation process, you have to enter some information which you can obtain from your Internet Service Provider (ISP) or from your network administrator.

For each new mail account you need these five details:

⇒ Your e-mail address

⇒ Your password

⇒ The name of your POP3 server

⇒ The name of your SMTP server

⇒ The name of your mail box

This might not mean a lot to you – but it will to your provider.

WHAT'S THIS?

POP3 server: used to **receive** mail

SMTP server: used to **send** mail

When you send mail you will frequently notice a strange character, an encircled a, the so-called 'at sign'. In an e-mail address this funny a separates the name from the location. Everything to the left of the at sign constitutes your e-mail name, and everything to the right of the sign your address that states your location.

It is very important that you enter e-mail addresses precisely. A letter addressed to 'Mrs Quen, Bucknghm Palce' will definitely be delivered to the Queen at Buckingham Palace. An e-mail message, however, in which as little as one letter is wrong, will definitely be returned as undeliverable.

Enough of the introductory remarks: let's start installing the e-mail account.

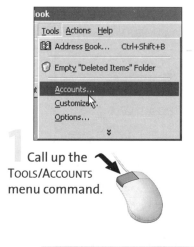

1 Call up the
TOOLS/ACCOUNTS
menu command.

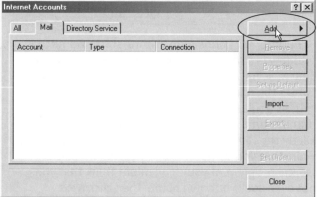

2 An empty Internet Accounts dialog box opens. You are
going to change this now.

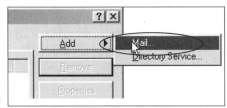

**3** Click *Add* and then choose *Mail*.

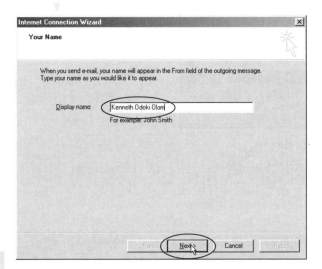

**4** The 'Internet Connection Wizard' starts. Admittedly  the window is almost empty, but do not worry, there is nothing missing, and your computer is not faulty either. First enter the name under which you are going to send e-mails. As a rule, this is the usual combination of first and family name. Your mail audience will see your name in exactly the same way as you enter it here. Therefore take care that you do not make any typing mistakes – or else the recipient of your mail might think that you cannot even spell your own name. Then click *Next*.

**Important!** Avoid any foreign language or other special characters, as they will be delivered as unreadable mumbo jumbo.

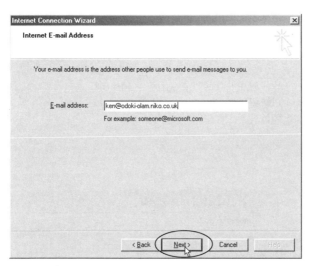

5 Next enter your e-mail address, which you will have received from your provider. Take care that you enter the address exactly as you have received it from your provider or your network administrator. Click *Next*.

You can type the @ sign by simultaneously pressing the [Alt Gr]+[Q] keys.

In the next step the mail servers are specified. These are special programs, which ensure that your electronic mail is sent correctly on its way through the network, and that the mail messages addressed to you really end up in your mailbox. Here too, you will have to enter the character sequence that you have received from your provider absolutely accurately.

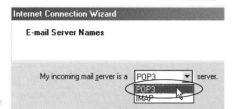

**6** First you have to enter the server type of the 'incoming mail server' by selecting the appropriate type from the list. It is an easy decision to make: if you do not know what to enter, take 'POP3'. It is the current default. If you had access to an IMAP server your provider would have explicitly stated this.

Incoming mail (POP3 or IMAP) server:

| mail.niko.co.uk |

**7** Enter the name of your incoming mail server (take care to spell it correctly!). This server is responsible for the management of your electronic mailbox.

An SMTP server is the server that is used for your outgoing e-mail.

Outgoing mail (SMTP) server:

| mail.niko.co.uk |

**8** The next field is for the name of the SMTP server, which is responsible for the correct sending and transferring of your e-mail.

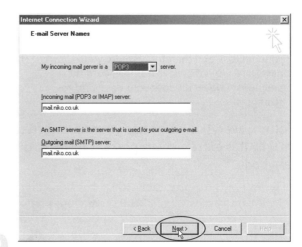

**9** As soon as you have filled in the three fields, click *Next*.

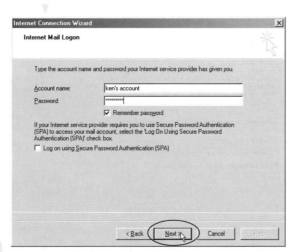

**10** After you have stated your address and the names of your two mail servers, you have to enter the name of your mailbox (that is the 'account name') and your password. The account name is almost always the same as the name in your e-mail address, that is the part which is on the left side of @ character. Sometimes it is the complete address – in this case your Internet provider will point this out to you.

There are tricksters who will tell you that they have to carry out important technical work on your mailbox and therefore require your password. Do not believe a single word these people say! Never disclose your password to strangers!

The combination of account and password is a little like a post-box with a key: just as everybody who has the key can open your post-box and read your letters, everybody who has your password can read your e-mails. That is why it is extremely important never to disclose your password to anybody.

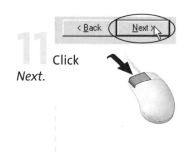

**11** Click *Next*.

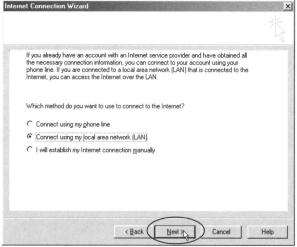

**12** Finally, you have to instruct Outlook, which method to use to connect to the Internet and therefore your mailbox. Choose the appropriate entry. Then click *Next*.

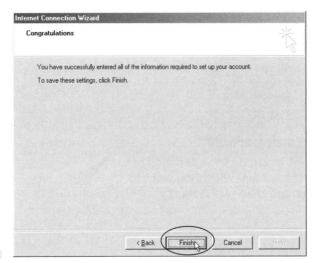

You have now completed all required entries. By clicking on *Back* you can again scroll through the various dialog boxes to check your entries. Clicking *Finish* concludes the procedure for the setting up of your e-mail account.

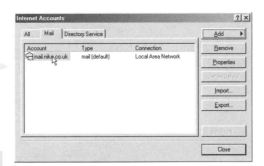

The newly created e-mail account is now displayed in the account list.

By default, Outlook enters the name of the POP3 server as the account name. This will usually not matter to you. However, as soon as you have several accounts, you should give them appropriate names so that you can remember them easily. This is how you do it:

**187**

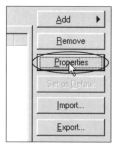

In the Internet accounts dialog box,
select the account which you want to
rename, and then click *Properties*.

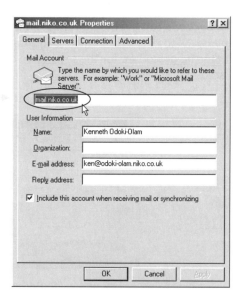

A dialog box consisting of several tabs
opens. We are only interested in the *General*
tab. Click in the top entry box.

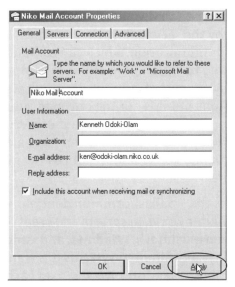

3 Type in the appropriate name. Then ensure that Outlook will record the name change by clicking the *Apply* button.

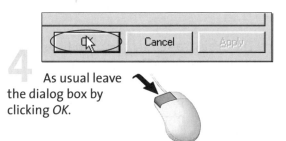

4 As usual leave the dialog box by clicking *OK*.

# Choosing the e-mail format

After the successful setting up of your e-mail account, you are now ready to send and receive e-mails with Outlook 2000. In principle this is very easy, but as so often happens, the little things cause all the problems. It is not unusual for your e-mail to arrive at its destination in Double Dutch.

**189**

Equally, it may happen that you send an e-mail in good faith which cannot be read by the recipient. The reason for this occasional breakdown in communication, which can completely put you off e-mails in the long run, lies in the different computer systems that are electronically connected. Admittedly Windows is the most common PC system, but it is not the only one. Always remember that just because you work with Windows and use Microsoft Office, it does not mean everybody else does, too. When you have used the Internet and e-mail frequently you will soon notice how many **different systems** there are.

Electronic mail is the smallest common denominator of the networked computer world. In spite of the great differences, for example, between **Macintosh, Windows, and Linux systems**, for users of these three basically different systems it is – almost without any problems – possible to send, receive and read each others e-mails. And that despite the fact that it is impossible to start Unix programs on a Windows computer or without tools to open Windows documents on a Macintosh.

Therefore, you have to ensure that your electronic mail complies with certain **rules**, so that the recipient can read it and does not simply see a mess on his screen instead.

Only if you are absolutely sure that you are sending your mail only to other Outlook users do you not have to modify the mail program. In all other cases it is imperative. The reason is that Outlook has a few peculiarities which work well if you are moving within the Microsoft Office world, but regularly cause significant misunderstandings as soon as you leave it. You will almost certainly leave this protected world as soon as you send electronic mail.

Therefore help yourself and your future mail partners: **change a few default settings** in Outlook 2000, and avoid possible misinterpretations. This is how you do it:

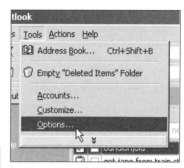

Call up the TOOLS/
OPTIONS menu command.

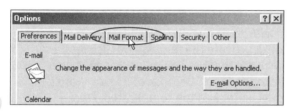

Activate the
*Mail Format* tab.

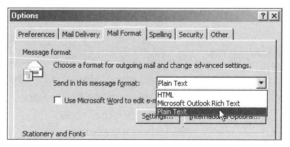

Choose the
'Plain Text' message
format.

**191**

If you choose HTML or Outlook Rich Text as a message format, you can send text with formatting such as *Italic* or **Bold**, and use colours and backgrounds, but you will run the risk that only Outlook users can understand you. It also means that you will send needlessly voluminous e-mails. However pretty these options may be, only use them if you are absolutely sure that the recipient approves of it.

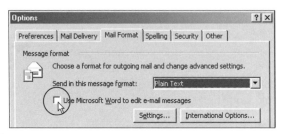

If the Edit *e-mail with Microsoft Word* field is activated (the box will be ticked), deactivate the function by clicking the check box. You can reactivate the function whenever you like, but as a rule it is not recommended. Because of its size, Word is too sluggish as an e-mail editor and too complicated. Word always makes a mail mountain out of each mail molehill.

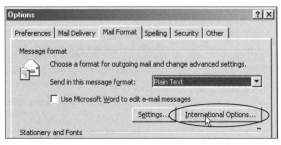

Now click the *International Options* button.

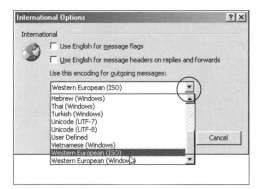

Check the coding settings. If necessary change them to 'Western Europe (ISO)'. Click the downward pointing arrow, and then choose the appropriate entry from the list.

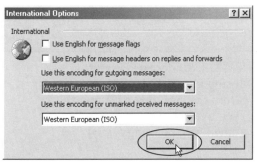

When you have chosen the correct coding, close the dialog box by clicking *OK*.

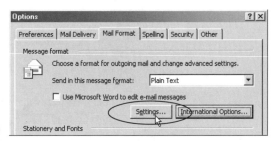

Once you are back in the Options dialog box, click the *Settings* button.

**193**

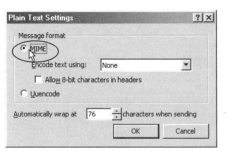

**9** Choose the MIME message format.

**MIME** is a special mail format, which permits the sending of files via e-mail. With '**Quoted Printable**' you can use foreign language and other special characters.

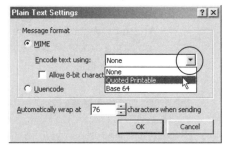

**10** Under Encode *text* using, choose 'Quoted Printable' from the drop-down list (which you open by clicking on the downward pointing arrow).

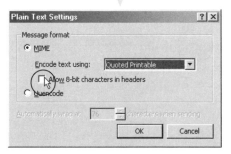

**11** If the *Allow 8-bit characters in headers* option is activated (check box is ticked), deactivate it by clicking in the check box.

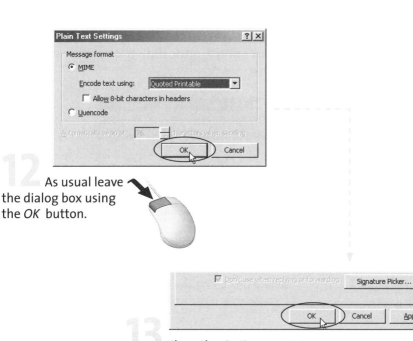

**12** As usual leave the dialog box using the *OK* button.

**13** Close the *Options dialog* box with the usual combination of *Apply* and *OK*.

# Signatures

On a letter, the sender tells the recipient who he/she is by writing his/her address in the top right-hand corner. There is nothing like that in e-mail messages. At the top of e-mail messages there is only a name and a meaningless e-mail address.

However, in e-mails there are 'signatures'. They are small scraps of text, which Outlook 2000 automatically adds to the end of e-mails. Signatures usually contain the sender's name and address, but may also be filled with little sayings, quotes, or jokes. What you put into a signature is up to you.

**195**

As Outlook can manage several signatures, you can create a whole range of signatures and choose one appropriate to the type of the e-mail message (private or business).

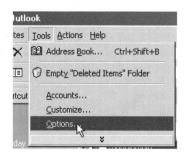

As you have done previously, open the *Options* dialog box using the TOOLS/ OPTIONS menu command.

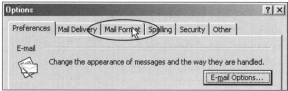

Choose the *E-mail Format* tab.

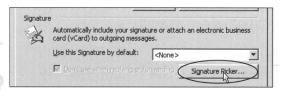

Before you can choose a signature, you first have to create one. Click the Choose *Signature Picker* button.

**196**

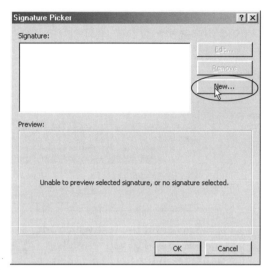

**4** The signature window is still empty. Click the *New* button.

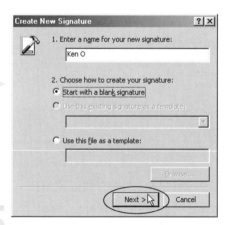

**5** Assign a name to the signature you are about to create. Then click on Next. The name is not part of the signature. Its only purpose is to facilitate signature management for you and Outlook 2000.

The first line, which separates the signature from the message, should consist of two dashes and a gap ('— '). In all, a signature should not consist of more than four to six lines.

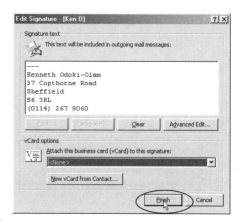

6 Now enter the text which you want to add to your e-mails a signature in the field box. Then click *Finish*.

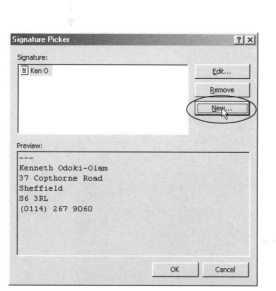

7 The newly created signature now appears in the list. In the preview window you can see the currently marked signature as Outlook will add it to your e-mail. Using New you can add further signatures, or close the dialog box using *OK*.

**8** Now you can choose your default signature in the *Option* dialog box.

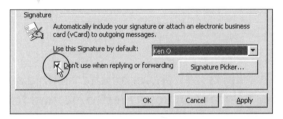

**9** It is recommended to activate the *Don't use when replying or forwarding* option. It prevents Outlook adding your signature to e-mails in which it is not needed.

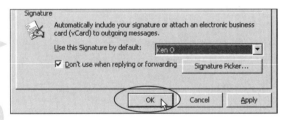

**10** Finally, close the *Options* dialog box using *Apply* and *OK*.

with e-mail

## What's in this chapter:

E-mail is just powerful and flexible as
it is inconspicuous. Electronic mail transfers
everything from a short note or discussion,
to a new printer driver as a file attachment.
This chapter teaches you the basic
knowledge required to use e-mail
successfully. You will
learn how to address,
send, and receive
e-mails, and what you
have to pay attention
to when you want to
send mail to several
people.

## You already know about:

## You are going to learn about:

# Writing e-mail messages

After you have installed your e-mail account and checked all your default settings, you are ready to send electronic mail with Outlook 2000. This is how you create a new e-mail message:

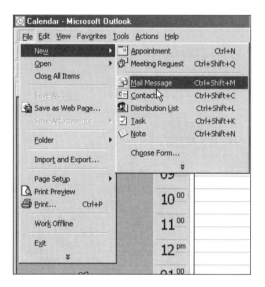

Open a new e-mail form by either calling up the FILE/NEW/MAIL MESSAGE menu command or by pressing the [Ctrl]+[⇧]up+[M] shortcut keys.

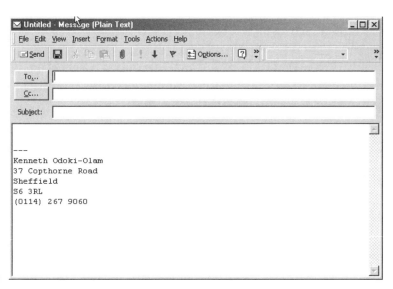

*2* In the new e-mail form that opens, Outlook enters the signature you defined and places the cursor in the address field.

The recipient's address has to be entered correctly. Even the smallest typing error renders the message undeliverable.

*3* Enter the recipient's e-mail address in the address field.

The recipient's address must be typed
correctly. Even the smallest typing error
renders the message undeliverable.

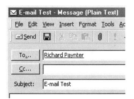

Click into the field under *Subject*, and
enter a keyword describing the contents of the
e-mail, so that the recipient can see what the
message is about. Make it as expressive as
possible, so that the recipient will be able to
guess at the contents of the mail message. If
your subject entry is insufficiently clear, it may
happen that the recipient deletes the message
without reading it.

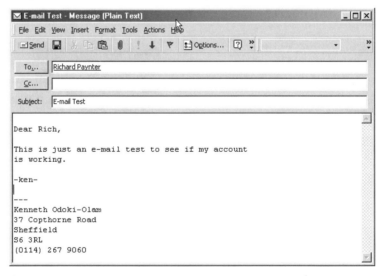

Now click in the big
empty box. This is the field
box in which you compose
your message.

6 When you have finished writing your message, click on the *Send* button. Outlook saves your message in the *Outbox* folder. Your electronic mail is now ready to be posted. You have, so to speak, sealed the envelope and stamped it, but it has not been sent yet

# Sending and receiving e-mail

When you close an e-mail message with *Send*, it will not be sent immediately, Outlook files it in the *Outbox* folder. You have to send the actual posting of your mail separately.

This may sound cumbersome, but it has a number of advantages. You cannot retrieve a mail message once you have sent it. The **temporary storage in the outbox** allows you to correct or modify the message later. Moreover, collecting your mail from your outbox has the advantage that you do not have to connect to the Internet for every new e-mail message you want to send. You can send all your mail at once instead. This saves you time, money, and hassle.

To open your outbox proceed as follows:

**1** On the Outlook bar click the 'My Shortcuts' entry.

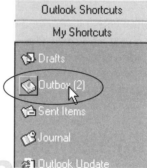

**2** Now open your outbox by clicking the corresponding symbol.

**3** The mail message – together with other messages – is still in your outbox waiting to be posted. If you now want to carry out any changes or check your message again, mark the mail message and open it with a double-click.

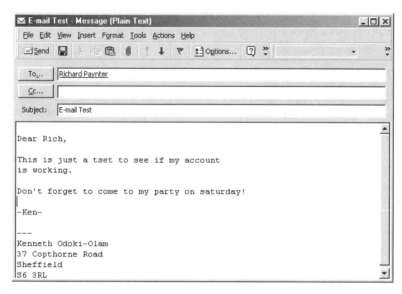

4 Double clicking opens the mail form.
You can now edit it.

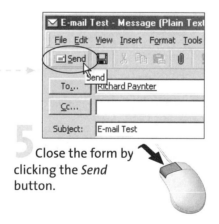

5 Close the form by
clicking the *Send*
button.

You can also close the mail form – like any other
window – by clicking the X in the top right-hand
corner. Caution! Although this procedure saves the
e-mail and all the changes you might have carried out, it will be
marked as a draft and will not be sent.

**207**

You can recognise a mail message that is ready for sending by two characteristics: its entry is in *Italics*, and it has a closed envelope as its symbol.

A mail message that is not ready for sending is not displayed in *Italics*, and has an open envelope with a page as its symbol.

As soon as you are happy with your e-mail it is time to send it.

**1** The easiest method is to post all your e-mail at once. Click the Send and Receive button on the toolbar, or press the F5 keyboard shortcut.

**2** Outlook now automatically executes the collection and sending of your mail for all registered e-mail accounts. Outlook checks your accounts in alphabetical order. If you want Outlook to check a specific account first, you have to select the relevant account name.

If you only want to send the waiting e-mails in your outbox, without having to go through the sometimes long-winded mail reception, you have to proceed slightly differently:

**1** Open the complete Tools menu by clicking the downward pointing double arrow.

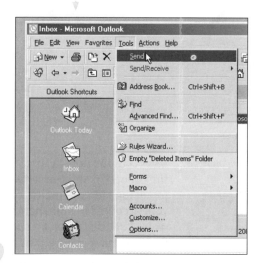

**2** Choose one of the newly added entries under the Send menu item.

209

You can also close the mail form – like any other window – by clicking the X in the top right-hand corner. Caution! Although this procedure saves the e-mail and all the changes you might have carried out, it will be marked as a draft and not sent.

Remember that you can recognise a mail message that is ready for sending because its entry is in *Italics*, and it has a closed envelope as its symbol. A mail message that is not ready for sending is not entered in *Italics*, and has an open envelope with a page as its symbol. As soon as you are content with your e-mail it is time to finally send it.

**1** The easiest method is to post all your e-mail at once. On the toolbar click the button Send and Receive, or press the keyboard shortcut F5.

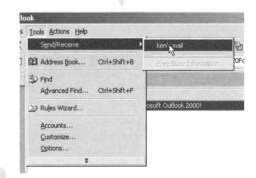

**2** Outlook now automatically executes the collection and the sending of your mail for all registered e-mail accounts. It checks your accounts in alphabetical order. If you want Outlook to check a specific account first you must choose that account name.

Just like any professional office, Outlook 2000 keeps copies of the correspondence: a copy of every e-mail sent is saved in the 'Sent Items' folder. Similarly to the inbox, you can call up this folder using the Outlook bar.

**1** Click on My
Shortcuts on the
Outlook bar.

**2** Then click
the *Sent Items*
symbol.

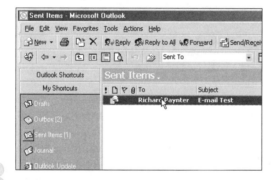

**3** Outlook then opens the corresponding folder, in
which all sent items (apart from mail messages,
Outlook can also send notes, appointments, and so on
by e-mail) are stored. From here you can move
important copies into other folders for archiving. We
recommend deleting everything else from time to time,
otherwise the folder will soon become too big and
messy.

# Sending mail to several recipients

A letter written on paper is always a unique document. You can send one specific letter only to a single recipient. Each time you want to send the same message on paper to several people, you have to copy the message appropriately and send a separate letter to each recipient.

This is made a lot easier with electronic mail. You can send as many copies as you want in a single pass. Simply insert several addresses instead of only one into the address field. Then you only have to separate each addressee from the other(s) with a comma or a semicolon.

There are many ways to send a mail message to several recipients. Technically they do not differ. They all result in all recipients receiving the same message. The differences are more a matter of discretion.

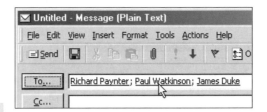

The easiest method: enter all the addressees into the 'To:' field of the e-mail. This means that all recipients have equal status. Depending on whom you are sending the message to, you should pay careful attention to the order of the names – some bosses might feel offended if their secretary were named before them.

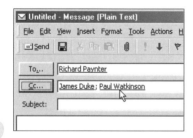

2 You can also distribute the addressees between the 'To:' and the 'Cc:' line. Cc stands for 'Carbon copy'. This distribution makes sense when the message is intended principally for the recipient/s in the 'To:' field, but you also want the other recipients to have a copy of the message you are sending. Here you should also think about the order in which you enter the addressees.

As a third and last possibility, you can enter addresses into the Bcc field. Bcc stands for 'Blind carbon copy'. A recipient listed under Bcc will also receive the message. However, only you and the recipient under Bcc will know about it. Before the mail is delivered to all the other recipients, the Bcc entry is deleted, so that there is no evidence of any additional recipient of the message sent.

Bcc promotes secrecy. Therefore it is problematic and you should avoid it if possible. This option only makes sense in very few cases, Outlook does not offer it as a default. You have to select it explicitly:

1 Open the extended VIEW options by clicking the downward pointing double arrow on the menu bar of the mail form.

**213**

2 Select the entry 'Bcc Field'.

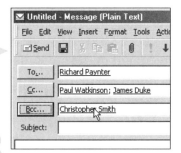

3 Now you can enter the addresses of the secret recipients in the Bcc field.

# Managing e-mail addresses

You can, of course, enter the addresses into the e-mail address field manually. However, this is a sure way of making mistakes and can be frustrating in the long run. Normally you would enter addresses using the address book; after all, that is what it is there for.

Open a new mail form.
Then click the *To*
button.

The address
books opens. Click
the appropriate
recipient, and insert
him/her into the
list of recipients by
clicking the *To*
button:

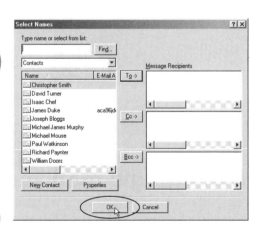

You can enter other
recipients in this way.
Then close the dialog
box using *OK*.

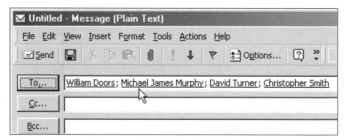

All these names have been entered into the address field. Now you can write and send your message.

If you frequently send mail and messages to a fixed set of people – such as a team in your company, or invitations to friends – you have to enter all the names each time. This is not only very laborious, but you may also easily forget an address. A useful tool is the **'distribution lists'**. Using this tool in Outlook, you can store several recipients under one name, such as 'Distribution List Friends'. When you eventually send mail to this particular name, it is forwarded to all recipients contained in the distribution list.

This is how you create a distribution list:

If the Contacts folder is not open, switch to it using the Outlook bar.

In the Contacts folder, call up the OPERATIONS/NEW DISTRIBUTI-ON LIST menu command.

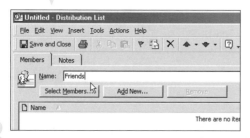

A form opens. First assign a name to the distribution list.

Then click the Select Members button...

**217**

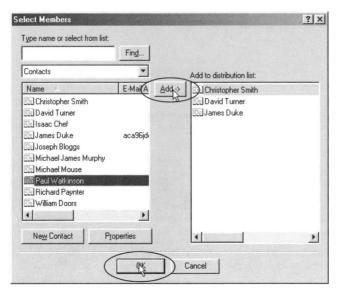

**5** ...and insert the individual names into the distribution list by clicking the *Add* button. Leave the dialog box using the *OK* button.

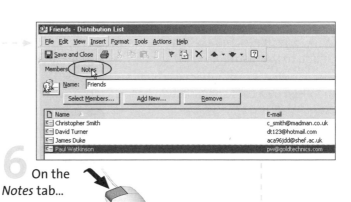

**6** On the *Notes* tab...

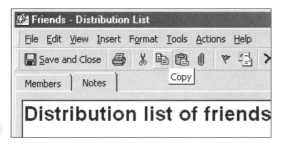

**7** ...you can add further details about the newly created distribution list.

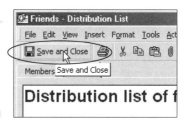

**8** Clicking *Save and Close*, adds the distribution list to your contacts order.

| | | | |
|---|---|---|---|
| | William Doors | LittleSoft | Doors, William |
| | James Duke | Cybertechnics | Duke, James |
| | **Friends** | | **Friends** |
| | Michael Mouse | Acme Cheese | Mouse, Michael |
| | Michael James Murphy | Murphy inc. | Murphy, Michael James |

**9** In the Contacts folder, you can recognise a distribution list by a changed symbol. A normal entry is marked with a stylised business card, whereas a distribution list is symbolised by a card showing two heads.

**10** From now on, you can enter the distribution list in the address field of a mail form. Each member of the distribution list will receive your mail without you having to enter each name separately.

**219**

If you want to add the addresses of friends into your address book, you can either fill in a new contact form or leave this job to Outlook. The prerequisite for this is that you have received at least one e-mail from your friend.

Open a mail message from the person you want to add to your address book either by double clicking it or by pressing the ⏎ key.

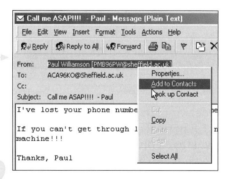

Right-click in the sender field, then choose the Add to Contacts entry from the context menu. Using the Find entry, you can check whether you have already entered this e-mail address under a different name.

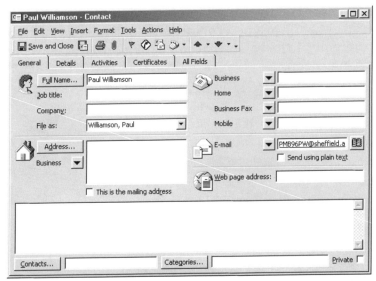

**3** Outlook opens a new contact form with the sender's name and the e-mail address. Here you can enter additional information. Finally, click *Save and Close*.

You may automate the adding of e-mail addresses almost completely, by instructing Outlook to automatically add every sender whose e-mail you reply to into the Contacts folder.

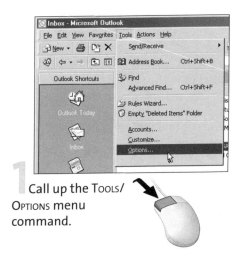

**1** Call up the Tools/ Options menu command.

**221**

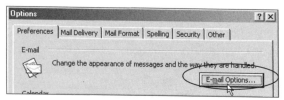

On the *Settings* tab, choose
the *E-mail Options* button.

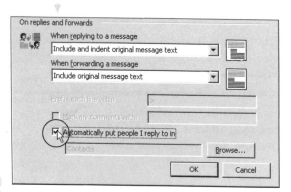

Activate the last entry at the bottom
(*Automatically put people I reply to in*) by
clicking the check box.

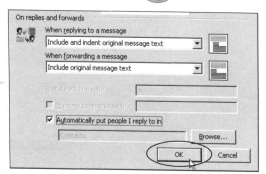

Close this and all the
remaining dialog boxes
with *OK*.

This option of automatically adding addresses is very useful, but it may lead to some confusion and even chaos within your Contacts folder. Since Outlook adds addresses of all contacts to whom you may have only written once, you should check your Contacts folder every now and again and delete all unwanted entries.

# Forwarding and replying to e-mail messages

Of course you will not only write e-mails and collect mail addresses, you will also reply to e-mails. This is how you do it:

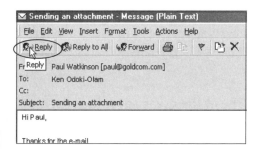

Open the mail message you want to reply to, then click the *Reply* button.

If you want to send your reply to all recipients of a mail message with several addressees, click *Reply to All*.

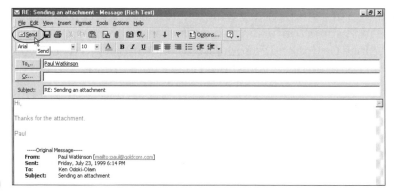

Outlook opens a new mail form. 'Re:' (standing for reply) is added to the beginning of the *Subject* field. The sender of the original message is entered as the new addressee. The complete text of the e-mail message you are replying to is inserted into the new mail message. The cursor is placed at the beginning of the message. You can now type your reply. Then click the *Send* button. Your reply is moved to your outbox.

One of the great advantages of e-mail is that you can forward messages to other recipients. In this way you can quickly inform other people about important information you have received.

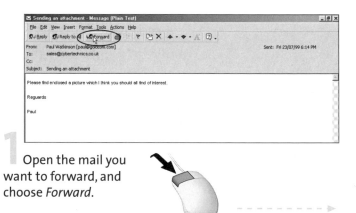

Open the mail you want to forward, and choose *Forward*.

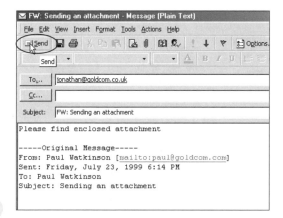

Again, the complete original mail message is copied into a new mail form. The cursor is placed at the beginning of the form. 'FW' (standing for forward) is added to the *Subject* field. Now enter the recipient of the message into the *To:* field. As usual move the message to your outbox using the *Send* button.

# File attachments

However, electronic mail can do more than just process text electronically. With e-mail, you can also send any file which is stored on your hard disk as a file attachment. No matter whether you have to send an Excel spreadsheet to your colleague at the next branch, a digitised photo of your family to friends overseas, or a useful utility to a business friend, you can do it using e-mail.

**1** Open a new mail form (using either the FILE/NEW menu command or the Ctrl + ⇧ + M keyboard shortcut).

**2** Call up the INSERT/FILE menu command from the mail form toolbar.

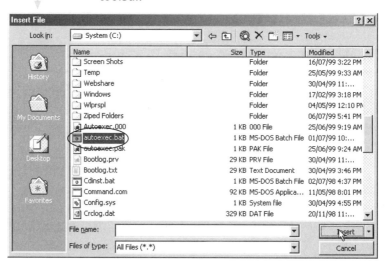

**3** A window opens. Choose the file you want to send and attach it to your e-mail by clicking the *Insert* button.

4 The attached file is displayed together with its symbol and name on a bar underneath the e-mail.

5 Now you can write – as in every other e-mail – your message, address the mail, and send it by clicking *Send*.

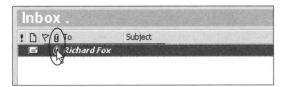

As you cannot tell at first glance what an e-mail contains, Outlook represents file attachments with a small paperclip.

Therefore, if you find a message with a paperclip in your inbox somebody has sent you a file attachment. However, you can only find out what the attachment is by opening the message and the attached file.

1 You can open such a mail message just like any other e-mail. You can open the attached file by double clicking the symbol.

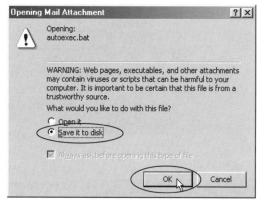

2 Outlook then asks you what you want it to do with the file. For safety reasons you should always choose the *Save it to disk* option. Select the appropriate operation by clicking *OK*.

However, you do not have to open an e-mail to have a closer look at the attachment.

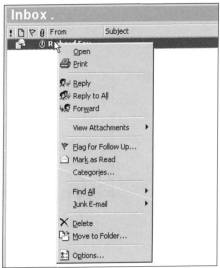

**1** Right-click the mail containing the attachment you are interested in.

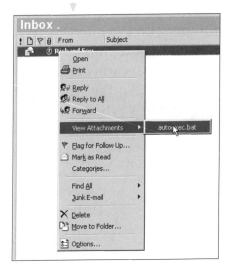

**2** Choose VIEW ATTACHMENTS and then the attachment you want to open.

# What's in this chapter:

Who is not familiar with those small, often square yellow scraps of paper, which you find stuck to monitors, documents, or calendars, in fact everywhere. Usually, they are hastily scribbled notes, containing phone numbers, and so on.

Admittedly,these notes are quite useful, but they have the uncanny tendency of disappearing just when we needed the phone number we just scribbled. This does not happen with Outlook notes. This chapter teaches you everything about these useful digital notes.

Ken's Web page
http://www.dcs.shef.ac.uk

don't forget to update this

20/07/99 05:03

# Creating notes

As with all other Outlook entries, you can also create notes using different ways such as the FILE/NEW/NOTE menu command or the toolbar.

However, there are two things that apply to a note: first it has to be quick. After all you do not want to have to scroll through menus and submenus just to take down a phone number. Secondly, you will need quick access to the function when the Notes folder is not active.

Therefore, we recommend memorising the shortcut key command for a new note properly, so that you can really use them. The keyboard shortcut always works in Outlook and is the quickest option available for opening a new note form.

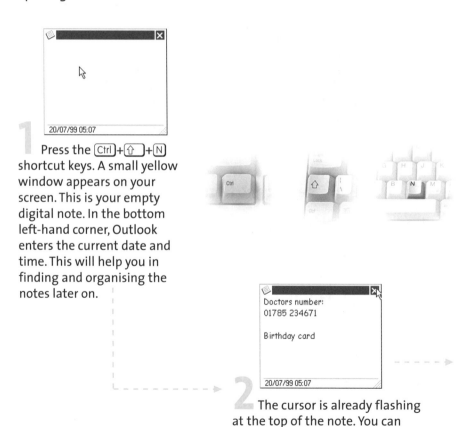

1 Press the Ctrl + ⇧ + N shortcut keys. A small yellow window appears on your screen. This is your empty digital note. In the bottom left-hand corner, Outlook enters the current date and time. This will help you in finding and organising the notes later on.

20/07/99 05:07

Doctors number:
01785 234671

Birthday card

20/07/99 05:07

2 The cursor is already flashing at the top of the note. You can simply start to type.

3 You can close notes as quickly as you can open them: just click the X in the top right-hand corner, or press (Esc).

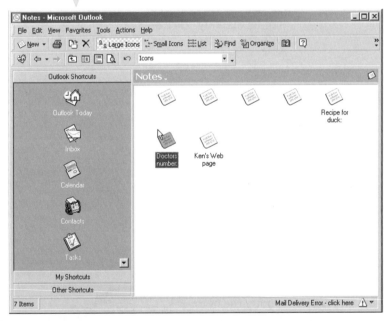

4 Each note, irrespective of whether you have written on it or not, is always stored in the Notes folder. In this way Outlook ensures that a hastily created note does not get lost in the hustle and bustle of everyday life.

# Formatting notes

However small a note may be, you have a range of formatting options with which you can display notes according to your liking.

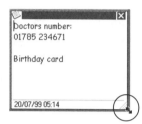

**1** At the bottom right you can see the Office-specific handle marking. Click on it with the mouse.

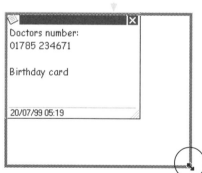

**2** Holding down the mouse button, you can modify the note to practically any rectangular shape and size by simply dragging.

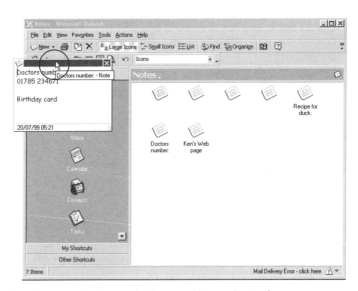

3 The individual notes are windows which are independent of Outlook. You can place them anywhere on your screen.

4 Clicking the small note logo in the left-hand corner...

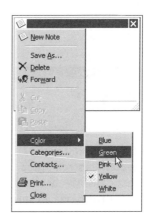

5 ....opens a menu in which you can, for example, change the colour of the note.

Using this menu you can also link the note to a Contacts folder entry. In this way you can directly access, for example, a required phone number from the note.

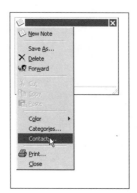

From the note menu choose the Contacts entry.

The contacts which are linked to the note are displayed. Using the *Contacts* button, you can select the entries you want to link.

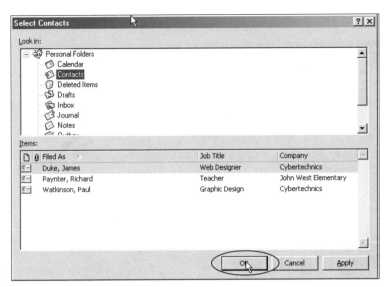

3 Choose the contact entry you want to link to the note. Then click *OK*.

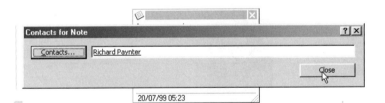

4 Exit the display of the linked contacts by clicking the *Close* button.

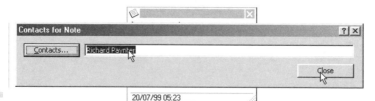

**5** If you want to access a linked contact, call up the contact display using the menu and double-click the name. Outlook then opens the corresponding contact form.

# Managing notes

Notes are always saved by Outlook, no matter whether you need the note again or not. This is very useful, but can lead to confusion in the Notes folder. We recommend regularly checking it and tidying it up.

**1** Open the Notes folder by clicking the corresponding symbol on the Outlook bar.

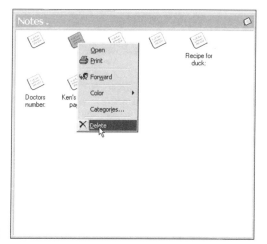

2 You can modify or delete notes by marking them individually and calling up the context menu by right clicking them.

If you use the notes frequently, the normal view of the notes can soon become very confusing. The VIEW menu offers help:

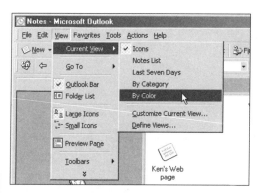

1 Using the VIEW/CURRENT VIEW menu command, you can specify the system under which you want the notes to be displayed. If you only want to see the current entries, choose LAST SEVEN DAYS. If you have up to now thought that the colour of the notes was a matter of personal taste, you are mistaken. Using the Color option...

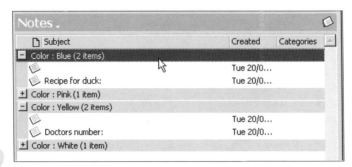

...you can sort the notes according to their colour. In this way you can establish a certain structure when you are creating notes.

# Modifying the default settings

If you do not like the default colour (yellow) and the default font for Outlook notes, you can change both.

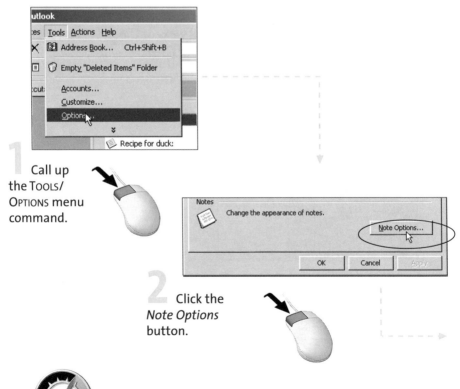

Call up the TOOLS/ OPTIONS menu command.

Click the *Note Options* button.

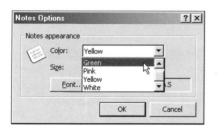

3 Here you can determine the default colour, font, and font size for the notes.

4 When you have finished your entries, close the dialog box (and all the following ones) with *OK*.

5 From now, on notes will be created with the font and the colour you have specified.

## What's in this chapter:

Loners are out; teamwork is not only more successful but also a lot more pleasant for all participants. With Office 2000 Microsoft supports teamwork via your Intranet or the Internet. Outlook 2000 is of course a part of this. Admittedly Outlook only develops its full capability for teamwork in connection with a Microsoft Exchange Server. However, even without it Outlook can support the shared project work in the team. This chapter teaches you the basics and how to send entries to colleagues, plan meetings, and delegate tasks.

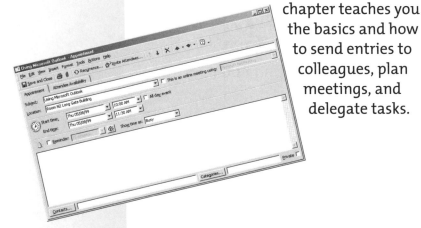

## You already know about:

## You are going to learn about:

# Sending Outlook entries

With Outlook 2000 you can send any type of files as attachments of an e-mail. This is very useful but not unusual. Almost every e-mail capable program can do that.

However, Outlook can do more. Namely it can forward entries from any Outlook folder by electronic mail. For example you can forward a complete contact entry with names, phone numbers, addresses, notes, and so on immediately and without any problems to a colleague, who can add the entry to his contacts folder with only a few mouse clicks.

The same works for notes, calendar entries, tasks, and so on. It does not matter which entry is in which folder – you can send it immediately by mail.

This is how you do it:

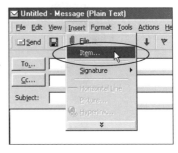

1 On the menu bar of the e-mail form choose the INSERT/ITEM menu command.

2 A dialog box opens. First determine the folder from which you want to send an entry...

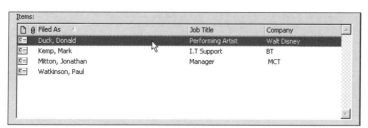

**3** ...and then the relevant entry.

**4** Make sure that the entry is inserted as an attachment.

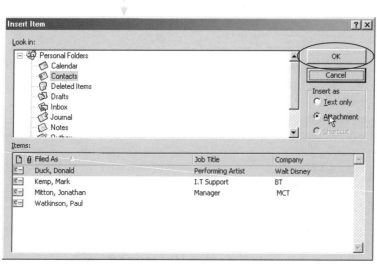

**5** Finally, click *OK*.

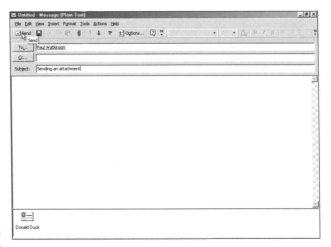

6 Now fill in the e-mail form as usual and click the *Send* button to see it off.

7 This electronic mail message, like any other, ends up in the recipient's inbox, where a paperclip icon indicates that there is an attachment. As in any other e-mail, it can be opened with a double-click.

8 Once the e-mail is opened, the recipient will recognise the symbol that indicates the type of file which has been attached to the mail message. With a double-click the appropriate form can be opened...

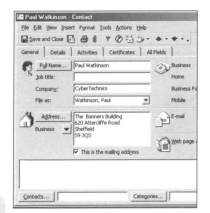

9 ...and the entry can finally be added to the database by clicking *Save and Close*.

However, remember that sending Outlook entries only makes sense if (and only if!) the recipient also works with Outlook 2000. Anybody else will only receive unreadable mumbo jumbo.

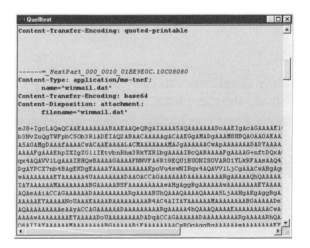

Content-Transfer-Encoding: quoted-printable

------=_NextPart_000_0010_01BE9E0C.10C08080
Content-Type: application/ms-tnef;
        name="winmail.dat"
Content-Transfer-Encoding: base64
Content-Disposition: attachment;
        filename="winmail.dat"

eJ8+IgcLAQaQCAAEAAAAAABAAEAAQeQBgAIAAAA5AQAAAAAADoAAEIgAcAGAAAAE1
b3NvZnQgTWFpbC5Ob3R1ADEIAQ2ABAACAAAAAgACAAEEkAYAMDgAAAM8HBQAOAAOAEAA
A5AGAMgDAAAfAAAAcwACAAEAAALACMAAAAAAHAJgAAAAACwApAAAAAADADYAAAA
AAAAFgAAAEnp2XIgZG1lIEtvbnRha3Rl3RkYXRlbgAAAAIBcQABAAAAFgAAAAG+nftDQxA
qx4AQAVVlLgAAAIBHQwBAAAAGAAAAFNNVPA6R19EQU1BUONI5OVAR01YLkRFAAsAAQ4.
DgAYPCX7nb4BAgEKDgEAAAAYAAAAAAAAAKpoVu4swNIRqx4AQAVVlLjCgAAACwABgAg
wAAAAAAAAEYAAAAA4UAAAAAAAADAAOACCAGAAAAAADAAAAAAAAARgAAAAQhQAAAAA.
IAYAAAAAAMAAAAAAABGAAAAABSFAAAAAAAAwAHgAggBgAAAAAAwAAAAAAAAEYAAAA
AQAeAA1ACCAGAAAAAADAAAAAAAARgAAAABUhQAAQAQAAAQAAAA5LjAAHgAKAGggBgA.
AAAAAEYAAAANoUAAAEAAAABAAAAAAAAB4AC4AIIAYAAAAMAAAAAAAAABGAAAAADe
AQAAAAAAeAAyACCAGAAAAAADAAAAAAAARgAAAA4hQAAQAAAEAAAAAAAACwA
AAAwAAAAAAEYAAAADoUAAAAAADADqACCAGAAAAAADAAAAAAAARgAAAARhQA
O4ATTAYAAAAAMAAAAAAAAARGAAAAABiFAAAAAACwROqAqqBqAAAAAAwAAAAAAAFV

# Meeting requests

Outlook proves its teamwork capabilities not only with the possibility sending of any type of entries, but also with the support it provides for typical teamwork tasks such as planning meetings. The full strength of the program can only be seen using a network with the Microsoft Exchange Server. However, even without this special server, Outlook is a useful tool, as long as all the participants work with Outlook. You can create meeting requests with the following procedure:

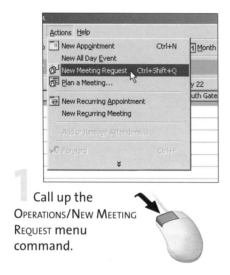

1 Call up the OPERATIONS/NEW MEETING REQUEST menu command.

Alternatively you can click the *Invite Others* button on the toolbar of the appointment form.

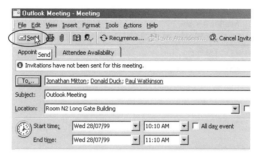

2 The normal appointment form becomes extended with an address field. As in a normal e-mail you enter the relevant recipients here, and hand over the request to your outbox by clicking *Send*.

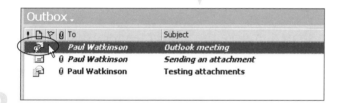

3 As in any other e-mail, a meeting request ends up in the recipient's inbox. However, this time the recipient can see immediately that it is not just a normal mail message when they see the meeting symbol.

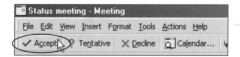

4 After opening the mail the recipient can decide whether he wants to accept the request or not, and enter the meeting into his calendar at the touch of a button.

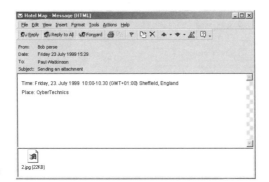

**5** This is what the request looks like when you send it to a recipient who does not read his electronic mail with Outlook. Therefore, take care in deciding to whom you send which message.

# Forwarding tasks

During work on a shared project, the project leader usually distributes the various tasks to the team members. It also often happens that somebody is delegated a task, only to find the next day that another team member would be better qualified to do the job. In such cases Outlook supports this teamwork with the delegating tasks function.

**1** To create a new task request, call up the OPERATIONS/NEW TASK REQUEST menu command.

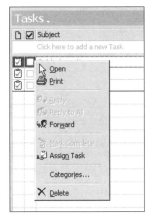

To forward an entry which is already in your task folder, right-click it...

...and choose the ASSIGN TASK entry from the context menu.

**251**

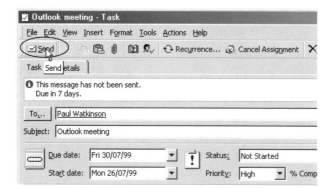

4 As previously in the appointment form, the task form is also extended by an address field. Apart from this it remains unchanged. You can fill it in as usual, enter the address, and post it with *Send*.

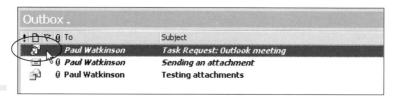

5 The task request ends up in the recipient's inbox. The symbol indicates that this entry is not a normal e-mail.

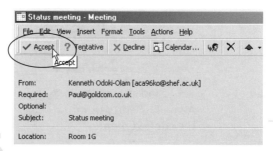

6 After opening, the recipient can accept the delegated tasks and add them to his task list or decline to do so.

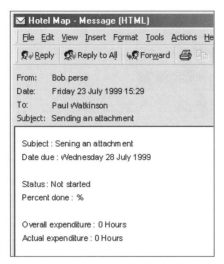

7 Do not forget that sending tasks only makes sense if the recipient also works with Outlook 2000. Otherwise he can merely read them and nothing more.

# Forwarding notes

If you want to send notes to your colleagues, for example because you have taken a phone call and want to give your colleague a message, you can simply send your Notes folder entry by e-mail.

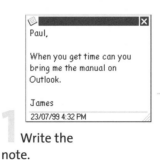

1 Write the note.

Then call up the notes menu by clicking the symbol in the top left-hand corner. Choose the FORWARD entry.

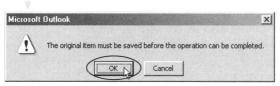

Outlook points out that the note will definitely be saved. Confirm the message with *OK*. Incidentally, this message is phrased slightly ambiguously. Outlook does not only inform you but also saves the note.

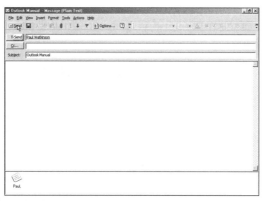

Outlook opens a mail form with the note as a file attachment. Now you can fill in the form and send it.

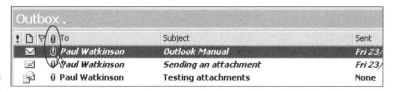

**5** In contrast to task and meeting requests, the recipient cannot recognise the forwarded note by a symbol, but has to open the mail to find out what it contains.

**6** It cannot be said often enough: this function should only be used if the recipient also works with Outlook 2000. Otherwise you confuse your mail partners with muddled stuff – and not every recipient will find this amusing.

# What's in this chapter:

Only a few years ago the Internet was only something for engineers, scientists, and researchers. Today there are hardly any areas in which the World Wide Web does not play a major role. The Internet and the communication techniques developed in it have a particularly powerful influence on all computer workstations and company networks. Outlook has not been left out, but is very much a part of this. This chapter teaches you how you can access the information offered on your Intranet or the Internet using Outlook, how to set up your homepage, and save important pages.

## You already know about: Creating tasks

## You are going to learn about:

# Accessing Web pages with Outlook

The close relationship between Outlook 2000, Office 2000, and Windows lets you access pages on the **Internet** AND **Intranet** from Outlook 2000 with no problems and without having to start Internet Explorer or any other Web browser.

However, before this is possible you must have activated the appropriate toolbar.

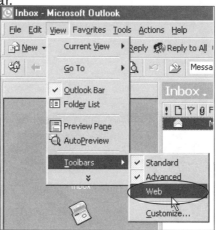

Call up the VIEW/TOOLBARS/ WEB menu command.

Alternatively you can right-click anywhere on the toolbar...

...and activate the Web toolbar.

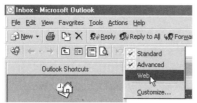

258

2 Type the Internet address of the page you want to visit in the field next to the globe. Press the ⏎ key once.

3 The page will be displayed in the current window – provided you are connected to the Internet.

# The Web toolbar

Using the symbols on the Web toolbar, you can control your Internet access. Perhaps you already know what all the individual symbols in Internet Explorer mean. However, it cannot do any harm to go over them again.

**1** With these two arrows you scroll backward and forward through the Web pages you have visited so far.

When pages are being downloaded very slowly, it sometimes helps to interrupt the downloading process and call up the page again.

**2** Sometimes the downloading of a Web page may take a long time. Using this button you can interrupt the downloading process.

**3** If the contents of a Web page have changed (for example in a current news service) Outlook might still be displaying the old version. By clicking on this symbol you instruct Outlook to reload the current page. In this way you ensure that you always see the most up-to-date information.

**4** Clicking the little house automatically connects you to your homepage or start page. You can specify your homepage in Internet Explorer (how this is done will be explained below).

The net is huge, You could say it is humungous. It contains an unimaginable amount of information and data. You only have to find it. When you click on the globe, Outlook downloads a Web page using various search engines to locate information on the Internet.

Finally, in this field box you enter the address of the Web page you want to view. When you press the ⏎ key, Outlook connects to the specified address.

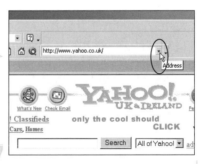

When you click the downward pointing arrow in the address field...

**261**

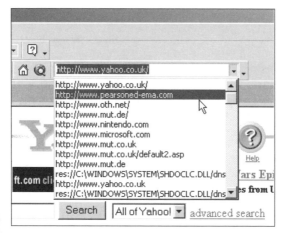

...a drop-down list of the addresses you have typed in so far opens. You can call up individual pages with a single click.

# Setting up the home page

By clicking the button in the shape of a little house on the toolbar, you instruct Outlook to download your homepage or start page. As default, this is a Microsoft information page. In the beginning, you can find some useful information here, but the information on the page soon loses its value. Why should you look at Microsoft adverts every day? However, this does not mean that the house symbol is not useful, as you can specify which page you want Outlook to display when you click this button.

Internet Explorer

To set your homepage you have to forget about Outlook for the moment and have a look at your Windows desktop. There you will find the symbol for Internet Explorer. Right-click it once.

Open
Explore
**Open Home Page**

Cut

Create Shortcut
Delete
Rename

Properties

**2** A context menu opens.
Choose the PROPERTIES entry.

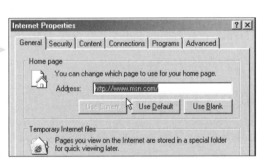

**3** In the *Properties* dialog box everything is automatically geared up to help change the homepage –
the entry in the *address* field is already highlighted for
you to overwrite as soon as you start typing.

**263**

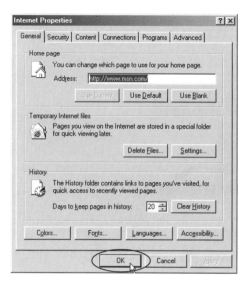

Enter the desired homepage address – such as the Intranet page for your company – and close the dialog box using *OK*. From now on when you click on the house symbol on Outlooks Web toolbar, you are taken to the newly specified page.

# Saving Web pages

As soon as you click any folder symbol on the Outlook bar, the corresponding folder opens. So far, so good. However, during activated Web access this can have fatal consequences: the currently displayed Web page is overwritten by the folder contents and there is no way to quickly get back from the folder to the Web page.

Fortunately, you can also create links to Internet pages on the Outlook bar. This is how you do it:

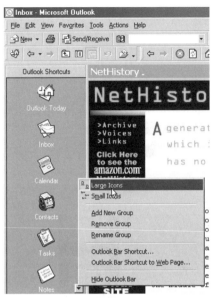

**1** Right-click the Outlook bar, which opens the context menu.

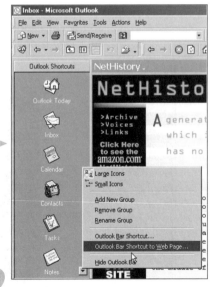

**2** Choose the OUT-LOOK BAR SHORTCUT TO WEB PAGE entry.

**265**

**3** Outlook informs you that a shortcut to the currently displayed Web page has been saved in *My Shortcuts*. Confirm with *OK*.

**4** When you now switch to the corresponding group on the Outlook bar,...

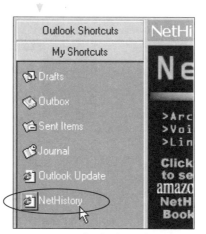

**5** ...you can see the link to the Web page as the last entry in the list. You can recognise a link to a Web page by the small Explorer symbol. Now you can call up a specific page on the World Wide Web.

Mostly these automatically created entries have names, which are far too long to be displayed on the Outlook bar. Furthermore, links to Web pages are rarely so important that you want to have them on your Outlook bar forever. In both cases the context menu of an entry provides help.

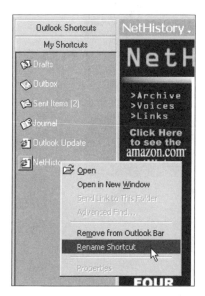

1 When you right-click the appropriate entry, the context menu opens. From here you can rename an entry...

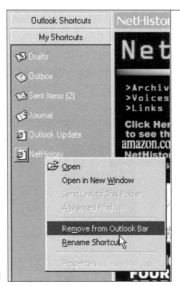

2 ...or delete it.

# 'The Favorites'

If you frequently access Internet or Intranet information with Outlook, you will soon notice that you want to save more and more interesting Web pages. When it gets to this stage, a link on the Outlook bar is not the best solution and will soon become overstretched.

Under these circumstances, you should make use of the *Favorites*. This is a main Windows directory, which can be accessed by all programs (that is, not only by Outlook but also by Word, Excel, Internet Explorer, and so on). All sorts of links to important files, documents, and Web pages are filed in here.

This has the great advantage that you can practically access your important data from every program. However, it can also very quickly create a messy chaos. When using the Favorites you should apply due care and attention from the outset, so that you can avoid being caught up in an undergrowth of different links and branches.

Download the Web page you want to save, and call up the FAVORITES/ ADD TO FAVORITES menu command.

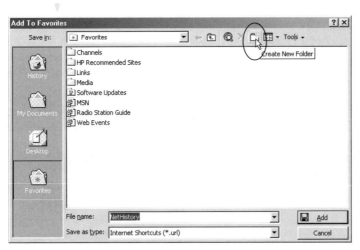

You can now enter the link by simply clicking on Add – but that will soon lead to chaos. You should instead file your Web links in a separate folder. Click this symbol to create a new folder.

**269**

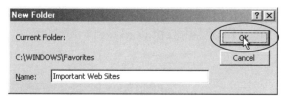

**New Folder**

Current Folder:

C:\WINDOWS\Favorites

Name: Important Web Sites

OK

Cancel

**3** Assign a name
to your new folder,
and click *OK*.

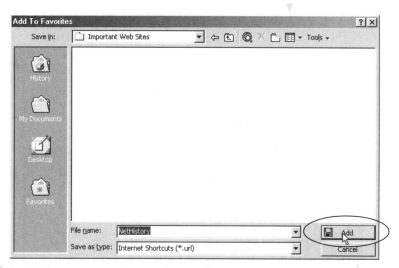

**Add To Favorites**

Save in: Important Web Sites     Tools ▾

History

My Documents

Desktop

Favorites

File name: NetHistory     Add

Save as type: Internet Shortcuts (*.url)     Cancel

**4** Outlook automatically switches to the newly
created folder. Now you can assign an easily
remembered name to the Web page. Click
*Add* to insert it into your Favorites collection.

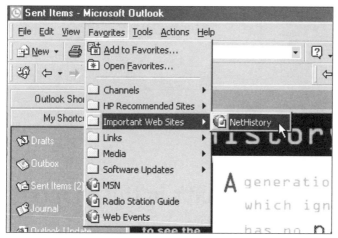

**5** In future you can quickly access your important Web pages from anywhere in Outlook using the FAVORITES menu.

## 12

## What's in this chapter:

This chapter deals with order. Data which is arbitrarily put together into one big pile does not constitute useful information, it is merely rubbish. To prevent this from happening in Outlook, this chapter informs you about how to find and sort data. You will also find out what categories are all about and take a behind-the-scenes look at Outlook's folder list.

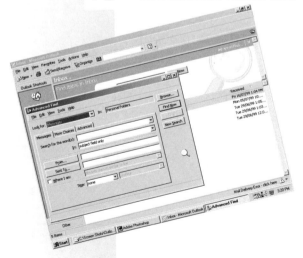

**You already know about:**

**You are going to learn about:**

# Basic search

In Outlook each folder has the option to search thoroughly and quickly for specific entries. How you do this is demonstrated below using the example of the inbox. The procedure outlined here can also be used without problems in all other folders.

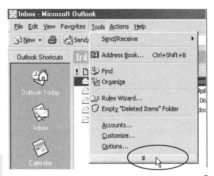

Call up the Find function by activating the extended menu with a mouse click on the double arrow and...

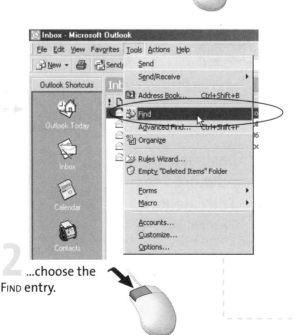

...choose the FIND entry.

**3** However, it is quicker simply to click the corresponding button on the toolbar.

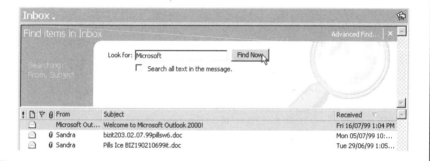

**4** In the top area of the folder display a window opens. Simply enter the word you are looking for in the text box. Which fields of the entry Outlook takes into account in the search is indicated in an almost unnoticeable fashion in light grey characters on a dark grey background in the left-hand area. In this example the entries in the folder 'Inbox' are searched for the word 'Microsoft' in the address and subject fields. Start the search by clicking on the Find Now button.

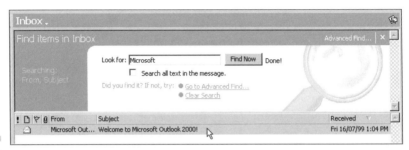

5 Depending on the size of the folders you are searching in, this process may take some time. To let you know what Outlook is doing, it displays the word 'Finished' next to the button. The search results are displayed below the search window. In this first attempt, we have extracted 92 e-mails from the inbox which contain the word searched for in either the address field or the subject field.

6 If you want to make sure that you do not miss any important entries, activate *Search all text in the message* (this removes the restriction of searching only in the address and subject fields) and start a new search.

7    To get back to the normal view of the folder you have to close the search window again. The easiest way to do this is to click the X in the top right-hand corner. As soon as the search window is closed, Outlook displays the inbox in its original view.

# Advanced search

The 'basic search' is always restricted to the contents of the currently active folder. However, what can you do if you do not know where the entry that you are looking for can be found or whether it exists at all?

In these cases the 'advanced search' can be used.

The 'advanced search' is a very powerful and complex full text search with a multitude of settings and parameters. But do not let this prevent you from using this search function. Many of its entries are only important in rather exotic contexts – just ignore these options.

As an example we will look for 'Picard' across all folders and entries.

1    As soon as the search window opens, you can activate the 'advanced search' by simply clicking the button.

**277**

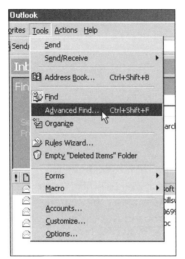

However, you can also choose the TOOLS/ADVANCED FIND command from the extended menu.

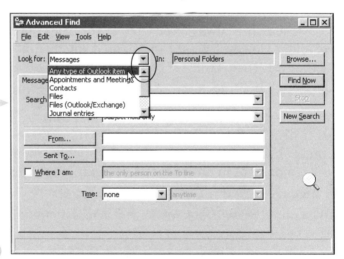

The extensive menu of the advanced search opens. First you have to specify which type of entry you are looking for. As we want to find everything with the term 'Picard' that has ever been recorded we choose *Any type of Outlook Item*.

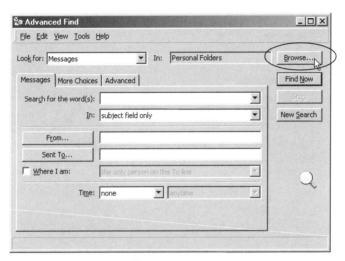

4 Open the menu using the *Browse* button...

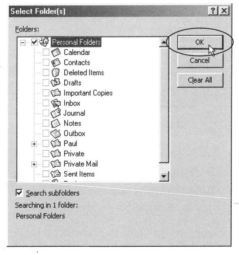

5 ...in which you can determine which folders you want Outlook to include in the search. When searching for all items, Outlook automatically switches to the highest folder level. Therefore you do not have to change anything here.

**279**

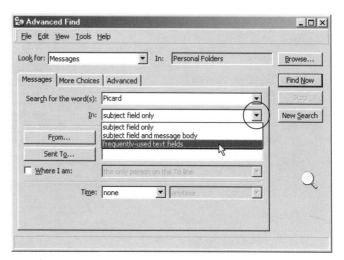

Finally, enter the search term ('Picard') and specify that you want Outlook to look in *Frequently-used text fields*.

When you click *Find Now*, Outlook begins searching. This may take some time, depending on the size of your Outlook database.

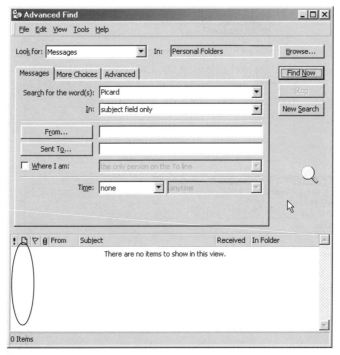

**8** After the search has been completed Outlook displays all the entries found. By means of the symbols you can see that Outlook has found notes, tasks, contacts, and e-mail messages. Therefore, it has really searched all available entries in all folders.

# The categories

You can assign any number of keywords – categories – to any Outlook entry, from inconspicuous notes, or appointments and tasks, to contacts entries. In this way it is possible to sort the different entries quickly and efficiently.

**1** You can assign different categories to new entries by simply clicking on the Categories button in the bottom right-hand corner of the form (at least for **contacts**, **appointments**, and **tasks**).

**2** To assign a category to a new mail message, either choose the VIEW/OPTIONS command on the menu bar of the message or click the *Options* button on the toolbar.

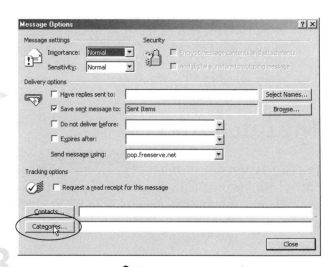

**3** A new dialog box opens, in which you can find the *Categories* button.

4 You cannot directly access the categories menu for new **notes**. To do this, you have to open the FILE menu by clicking on the small note logo in the top left-hand corner. In this menu choose the CATEGORIES entry.

5 You can also assign a category to a previously saved entry. Right-click the entry and choose the CATEGORIES item from the context menu.

In the **categories** window you can choose from comprehensive list – the only real disadvantage is that in practice the list provided is completely useless. Can you see any particular structural advantage in assigning (as general as they are useless) keywords such as 'Holiday', 'Ideas', 'Strategies', or 'Suppliers' to your notes, mail messages, and appointments? Consequently, you have to delete it and create your own categories list before you can use it in any useful way.

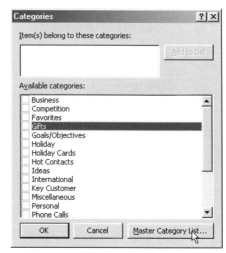

This is how you do it:

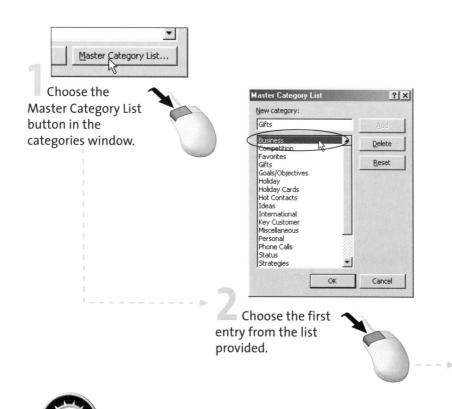

Choose the Master Category List button in the categories window.

Choose the first entry from the list provided.

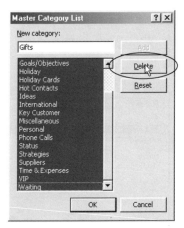

3 Hold down the ⬆ key and click the last entry of the list. In this way you mark all entries. You can release the ⬆ key and remove the complete list with Delete.

TIP

In the unlikely event that you prefer to work with the categories provided, choose the *Reset* button. This undoes all changes you have made in the list and restores its original state.

Now you can enter the keywords and categories that are really useful for your work and will actually help you in organising your entries.

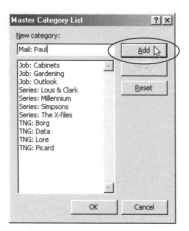

1 Enter your keywords into the field box, and one by one insert them into the list by clicking the *Add* button.

2 Close the dialog box with *OK*.

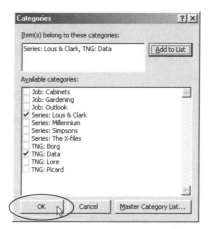

3 When you now open the categories window of an entry, you can assign your own categories to your entry.

Categories are of course not useful by themselves, but are supposed to help you to find related entries in different folders quickly and efficiently. If, for example, you assign a corresponding category 'Tax' to all the entries related to your tax return, you can extract them from the jumble of data from your Outlook database with only a few mouse clicks.

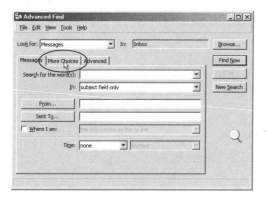

1 Start the *advanced search* (shortcut keys: [Ctrl]+[⇧]+[F]). Search for all Outlook items and choose the More Choices tab.

**287**

**2** Call up the categories list using the *Categories* button.

**3** Choose the appropriate category. Confirm your choice using *OK*.

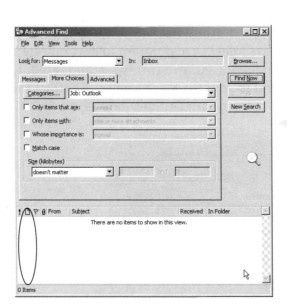

**4** After the usual click on *Start*, Outlook collects the different entries.

# The folder list

Outlook manages all information, from the hastily scribbled note to the important e-mail message, in folders. You are already familiar with this type of folder from Windows Explorer.

The folder list is there to help you work with these folders. The Outlook bar only ever works with links, whereas you can directly access the folders using the folder list. This has some advantages but also disadvantages: when you delete a link on your Outlook bar, the folder still exists – accidental deleting does not result in data loss; however, this is different for the folder list. Here you directly manipulate the folder and it may happen that you accidentally delete, move, or damage a folder. Navigating Outlook using the folder list can therefore only be recommended to experienced Outlook users. It is only explained here for reasons of completeness.

The folder list is normally invisible. Outlook only displays it for particular operations such as the creation of new folders. To call up the folder list proceed as follows:

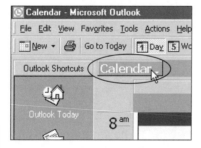

**1** In the folder display you can see a downward pointing arrow next to the folder name. It indicates that you can proceed here by clicking it. Follow this clue and click the name.

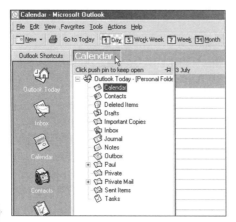

The folder list with the directory tree of the various Outlook folder opens. You can now work with the list. You can, for example, create a new folder. As soon as you click on an outside area, Outlook closes the folder list.

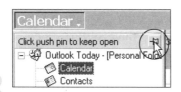

To permanently display the folder list, click the pin in the top right-hand corner of the folder list.

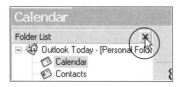

The pin turns into an X with which you can close the list – like any other window in Windows.

If, after some practice, you prefer to work with the folder list instead of the Outlook bar, use the following much quicker way to activate the folder list.

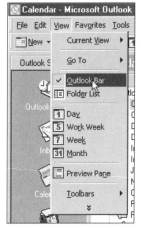

1 Call up the VIEW/FOLDER LIST menu command. Outlook then permanently places the folder list next to the Outlook bar.

2 Now you can hide the Outlook bar using the VIEW/OUTLOOK BAR menu command.

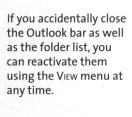

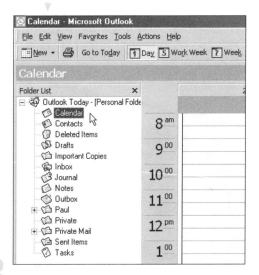

3 You can access all folders using the folder list, just as you can using the Outlook bar (here for example, the calendar).

**291**

# 13

## What's in this chapter:

Muddle makes trouble is how the saying goes. This may be a little exaggerated, and Outlook even allows for some creative chaos, thanks to its elaborate and powerful search functions. Nevertheless, you should keep everything neat and tidy, to prevent chaos from taking over. Outlook supports you in this task by offering important organisational functions, especially for mail management. In this chapter you are going to learn how to organise your inbox, restore accidentally deleted entries, and compress your Outlook database.

## You already know about:

## You are going to learn about:

# Organising

There are three main tools that ensure a clear structure and overall neatness in Outlook: firstly, there are **categories** for the classification of individual entries; secondly, there are **folders** for storing similar and related entries; thirdly, there are **folder views** with which you can display the contents of a folder in different combinations to cater for different needs and different information.

 These three options can not only be accessed individually using the corresponding menu items, but also using the 'Organize' function. You can call up this function either using the extended menu bar in Tools/Organize or by clicking on the corresponding button on the toolbar.

This function is a classical case of deceptive appearances. When you click on the button an important-looking window with various drop-down lists, menus and 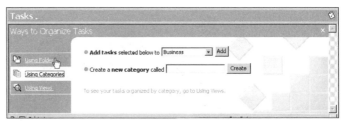 buttons opens. However, on closer inspection you soon discover that it merely offers you functions which you can access much more easily and quickly using the menu bar: moving entries into other folders, assigning categories to entries, and changing the folder view.

Which possibilities are available in the window depends on the currently active folder. In principle *Organize* offers you access to the folder list, the categories, and the views. The following table tells you from where you can access what:

|          | Views | Folders | Categories |
|----------|-------|---------|------------|
| Contacts | Yes   | Yes     | Yes        |
| Calendar | No    | Yes     | Yes        |
| Tasks    | Yes   | Yes     | Yes        |
| Notes    | Yes   | No      | Yes        |

In none of these folders does *Organize* offer you functions that you cannot access more easily, quickly and efficiently using the menu bars or the toolbars.

Therefore, this function is a completely superfluous gadget – until you use it in your inbox. Here *Organize* offers new and very useful possibilities to cope with the daily flood of data.

# Organising the inbox

The more you work with **e-mail** the quicker you realise the vast usefulness of it.

The only disadvantage is that if you use it a lot your inbox soon resembles a cluttered storage room.

However, Outlook can even help you with this.

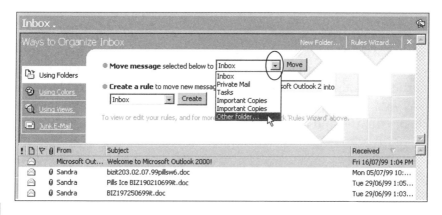

1 Open the organisation field either by calling up the TOOLS/ ORGANIZE menu command or using the corresponding button on the toolbar. On the *Use folders* tab you can specify to which folder you want to move the currently active mail message. The field box always displays the last used folder. If the folder you are looking for is not in the list, choose *Other folder* to access the folder list in which you can create a new folder.

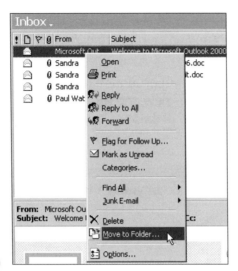

2 This is quite nice but not particularly exciting. It is a lot easier and quicker to move individual entries by calling up the corresponding menu with the right mouse button, as explained in detail in Chapter 3.

By contrast, the next point is really important: **creating a mail rule.** Here you can determine that mail messages from particular senders or to particular addresses are automatically moved to specific folders. In this way your inbox is automatically pre-sorted by Outlook. This promotes clear structure and transparency in the info jungle.

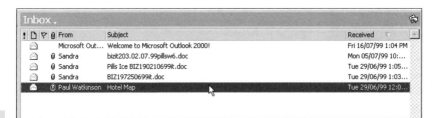

1 Mark any mail message from the sender which you want to filter out of the daily flood of data.

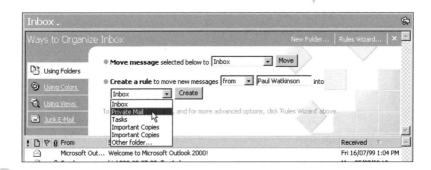

2 Then click on the *Organize* button and specify the folder into which you want Outlook to move any future mail messages automatically.

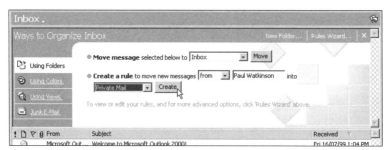

**3** When you click on *Create*, Outlook files the new mail rule according to which all new mail is automatically filtered.

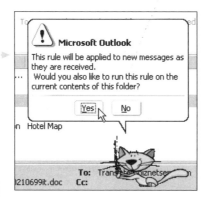

**4** The office assistant pops up and asks you whether you want to apply the new rule to the currently active folder now. Click on *Yes*, after all you do want to tidy up your inbox.

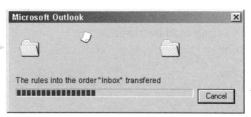

**5** Outlook now searches the inbox and moves all the mail messages which comply with the newly created rule.

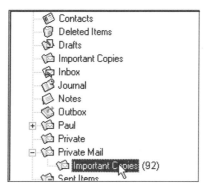

6   In this example 92 e-mail messages have been moved from the inbox to their appropriate folder.

However, sorting e-mails into various folders is not the only thing you can do. You can also automatically mark mail messages in different colours. In this way you can see at a glance whether you have received mail from particular people.

1   Open the
*Using Colours* tab...

...and assign a colour to the
sender. After clicking the *Apply
Color* button ...

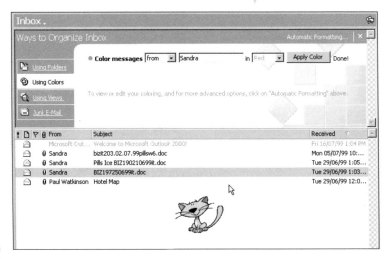

...all mail messages from the selected sender are marked in
the chosen colour (it is not very convincing on a black and white
printout, but very effective on a colour monitor).

# Restoring deleted entries

When you delete an Outlook entry, it does not disappear completely, but is temporarily moved to the 'Deleted Items' folder. Only if you delete an item in this folder, it will be permanently removed from the Outlook database. This has the advantage that you can retrieve accidentally deleted addresses, messages, or whatever from the recycle bin.

And this is how you do it:

*1* Click once the recycle bin, which is the symbol for 'Deleted Items'. As for every other link on the Outlook bar the corresponding folder is subsequently displayed.

*2* Using the different symbols, you can recognise what the various entries are: tasks, notes, mail messages, and so on. If you detect an accidentally deleted entry (in this example, an address entry), call up the context menu of the entry by right clicking. Then choose the MOVE TO FOLDER command.

**301**

Outlook opens the folder list from which you choose the target folder. As in this example we are dealing with an address, choose the Contacts folder. Clicking *OK* instructs Outlook to move the deleted entry from the recycle bin to the specified target.

# Permanently deleting entries

From time to time you should permanently empty the recycle bin, so that your Outlook database will not contain more rubbish than information.

Remember: The entries will be permanently deleted. You **cannot** restore them!

Right-click the bin symbol and choose the EMPTY DELETED ITEMS FOLDER option.

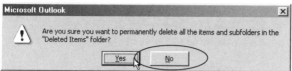

**2** When you confirm with *Yes,* Outlook permanently moves the contents of
the recycle bin into the digital nirvana.

You can also automate the deleting process, so that the bin is
emptied upon exiting Outlook.

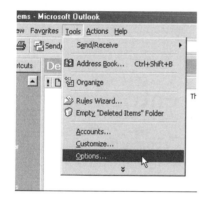

**1** Call up the
TOOLS/OPTIONS
menu
command.

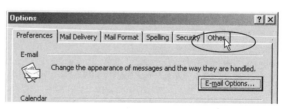

**2** Activate the
*Other* tab in the
Options dialog box.

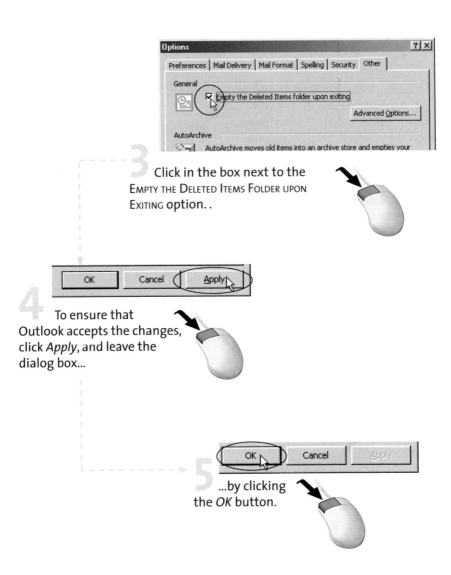

**3** Click in the box next to the EMPTY THE DELETED ITEMS FOLDER UPON EXITING option..

**4** To ensure that Outlook accepts the changes, click *Apply*, and leave the dialog box...

**5** ...by clicking the *OK* button.

# Tidying up Outlook

The more you work with Outlook, the more you will value it. Outlook manages your addresses and appointments, you send and receive mail messages with Outlook, archive your notes and documents with it, and so on.

However, do not enter your data to store it in Outlook unchanged until the end of time. Work with your entries! A business partner moves house, so you have to update the addresses of your contacts. You do not have to keep every note. You can move entries between the folders, store mail, so on and so forth.

This has two effects: firstly, your Outlook database grows bigger and bigger, and secondly the database is soon rather messy. You could just ignore this, but the messier your files are, the longer Outlook takes to search them. Soon it is like on a messy desk – looking for the required information takes longer than the actual work you have to do with it.

It is high time to tidy up. Depending on how intensively you use Outlook you should tidy up its data records once a week or once a month. Fortunately this is significantly easier in Outlook than it is on our desk. In Outlook the computer does all the laborious tidying.

As in real life you start by throwing away superfluous things. Correspondingly, in Outlook you start by emptying the recycle bin (see above). After you have taken care of the rubbish, you can tell Outlook to start tidying.

Right-click the 'Outlook Today' symbol on the Outlook bar. In the context menu choose the *Properties* item.

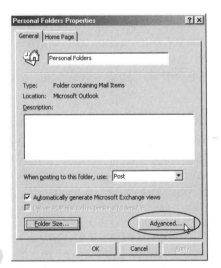

## 2 Click the
right-hand button
*Advanced*.

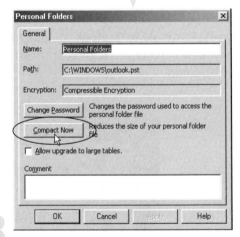

## 3 A further dialog box opens.
Click *Compact Now*.

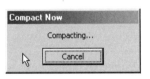

## 4 After Outlook has
compressed the file...

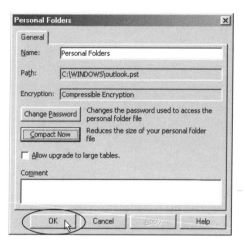

**5** ...click *OK*.
You return to...

You should regularly compress your Outlook database. As a consequence Outlook will work more quickly and reliably.

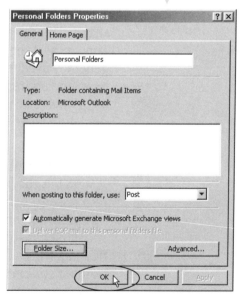

**6** ...the *Properties* dialog box.
Leave it by clicking *OK*, too.

**307**

**Account**　➠*E-mail account.*

**Assistants**　Small help programs which are supposed to facilitate working with programs such as Outlook or Word. When asked to, they explain particular operations, such as the saving of documents, step by step.

**BCC**　Abbreviation for 'Blind Carbon Copy'. A method of addressing ➠*e-mail*, similar to ➠*CC*. Normally the recipient of an e-mail message is shown. This does not apply to BCC entries. Here it appears as if the e-mail had no recipient. BCC is generally used for mail messages, which are sent to several addressees, if you do not want the recipients to know to whom you have sent the mail message.

**Binary System**　Number system with which a computer calculates. The common decimal system has the number ten as its basic unit and recognises ten different digits from 0 to 9. A computer can only distinguish between two states: electricity is flowing, electricity is not flowing. Thus a computer works internally with a number system which has a basic unit of 2. It only knows two different digits, 0 and 1.

**Bit**　The smallest information unit of a computer. A bit can represent two states: 0 and 1, electricity is flowing, electricity is not flowing. 8 bits are equivalent to one ➠*byte*.

**Browser**    Program for displaying information on the ➠*Internet*. As browsers were originally designed to display Web pages, while the Internet consists of more than just the ➠*World Wide Web*, a browser is also often referred to as Web browser. The two most important Web browsers are the Microsoft Internet Explorer and the Netscape Navigator.

**Byte**    A central information unit in computers. A byte consists of 8 ➠*bit* and can mark $2^8$=256 different states. In computers the management of a letter requires one byte.

**Categories**    Keywords which can be assigned to an Outlook entry to make it easier to filter entries, such *as* ➠*e-mail* messages, notes, or tasks, which are structurally different but similar with regard to their contents.

**CC**    Abbreviation for 'Carbon Copy'. A method of addressing ➠*e-mail*. The CC recipient receives a copy of the e-mail. Technically it does not make any difference whether recipients are entered in the To or the CC field, they will receive the same mail message. CC addressing is frequently used when a mail is sent to the direct addressee and for the attention of other recipients.

**Client**    Counterpart of a ➠*server*. A client is a special computer program, which processes the data of a corresponding server in a network. Thus, a ➠*browser* is a client which displays the data of a Web server, and a mail program is a mail client which receives ➠*e-mails* from a ➠*mail server*. Often individual machines are also referred to as clients, for example, a workstation in a network. This, however, is not quite accurate, as the network program running on the machine is the client and not the machine.

**Context menu**    When you right-click any area in Windows 95/98 or in a Windows program, (almost) always a so-called context menu opens. In it you can directly access currently possible operations. The contents of the menu change depending on the screen area and the program context.

**Copying**    When copying text or files the original text or file remains unchanged, and at the target (that is the place to which you copy) an exact copy of the original file is created. ➠*Moving*.

**CPU**    Abbreviation for Central Processing Unit – also referred to as processor. The CPU crucially determines the power and the possible applications of a computer. A Windows computer almost always works with a CPU of the producer Intel.

**309**

**Database**   A collection of several ➡*data records*, which are managed by a program. A database is the electronic equivalent of a card-index box, in which, for example, customer addresses are managed on individual index cards.

**Data record**   If a ➡*database* is a card-index box, then a data record is an index card. A data record consists of individual ➡*fields* such as 'Name', 'First Name', 'Place', 'Postcode', and so on. A collection of data records constitutes a database.

**Desktop**   Figuratively speaking the desktop in Windows 95/98 is the surface displayed on your screen on which individual symbols, folders, and files are placed.

**Download**   In the traditional schematic display of a network the central computer – the network server – is placed at the top, whereas the workstations (➡*client*) are grouped at the bottom. When data is sent from the server to the client, it flows from the top to the bottom. This is referred to as 'downloading'. If, on the other hand, data is sent from a client to the server, it is uploaded.

**Drag & Drop**   Central operating element in Windows and other graphical user ➡*surfaces*. Symbols, icons, or marked entries and text passages are grasped with the mouse, moved to a different place, and released. In this way it is possible to move or copy, for example, Outlook entries by means of drag & drop. It is also possible to move text onto the printer symbol and thus print it out.

**E-Mail**   Electronic mail. Instead of sending a message on a piece of paper, e-mail sends a text as a file in electronic form. To read and write e-mail, an e-mail program or a program, like Outlook, which provides the appropriate functions is required.

**E-Mail account**   Outlook manages all the data that are required to send and receive ➡*e-mail* in an e-mail account. Such an account has to be installed separately, before it is possible to use e-mail with Outlook.

**Event (in the calendar)**   An appointment which lasts one whole day (for example a conference).

**Exporting**   When data are converted from one ➡*file format* into another format, and are then saved in that new format, the data are 'exported' into a different format. Example: The saving of a word document in ➠*Rich Text Format* instead of Word format. ➠*Importing.*

**Fields**    A field is the smallest unit of a ➠*data record.* If a ➠*database* is a card-index box, and a data record is an index card, then the field is an entry on an index card. A data record consists of individual ➠*fields* such as 'Name', 'First Name', 'Place', 'Postcode', and so on. Every ➠*folder* in Out-look represents a database, and every entry in a folder corresponds to a data record. Every entry consists of individual fields.

**File format**    Whether text, image, video, or sound: to the computer all of these files are merely collections of data. Only if the data are presented in a particular structure and sequence – that is if they have a specific format – can they be processed by programs. Every program uses its own format. A contact entry in Outlook can only be read with Outlook, and an Access database only with Access. To be able to exchange data between different programs the file formats have to be adapted. This process is called ➠*importing* or ➠*exporting.*

**Folder list**    Hierarchical list of all folders available in Outlook. Normally it is not visible and can be displayed in different ways, for example via the menu command VIEW/FOLDER LIST.

**Folders (in Outlook)**    Outlook stores all information in entries and these entries in turn in folders. Folders can only store one specific entry type; the Contacts folder only contains contacts, the Notes folder only notes, and the Tasks folder only tasks. In Outlook a folder corresponds to a ➠*database,* and an entry to a ➠*data record.*

**Form**    Outlook uses different forms to record and display data. On these forms the individual ➠*fields* of the respective entries (➠*data record*) are placed. A form ensures that every entry in the ➠*folder* is displayed in the same way.

**Gbyte**    The next biggest unit after ➠*Mbyte.* It is often wrongly referred to as gigabyte. 'Giga' however is a term used in the decimal system and means a billion times ($10^9$). Thus a gigabyte would correspond to 1,000,000,000 ➠*bytes.* As a computer calculates with the ➠*binary system* this value is not correct, but too small. 1 Gbyte=1,024 Mbytes =1,024*1,024 Kbytes=1,024*1,024*1,024 bytes=1,073,741,824 bytes.

**Hardware**   All parts of a computer that can be touched: diskettes, power supply unit, graphics card, memory units, and so on. This also applies to the so-called peripherals such as printer, mouse, keyboard, or monitor. To be able to use the hardware, you require ➠*software*, which on the one hand ensures that, for example, the electronic pulses that are generated when pressing the keys on a keyboard are turned into a character on the screen (➠*operating system*). On the other hand you need the actual programs with which you can use the letters which have been generated on your screen for writing, for example a text processor.

**Homepage**   Almost always used to refer to the start page of an Internet offer. In Outlook you can also assign a homepage, which is always displayed when you switch to the ➠*folder*, to the individual folders.

**HTML**   Acronym for ➠*Hypertext Markup Language*. It is often wrongly referred to as a programming language. HTML is a so-called markup language which, independent of any specific program or any particular computer, defines the appearance of a screen page. All pages on the ➠*World Wide Web* are default coded in HTML. Therefore the pages look similar on different computer systems: bold is always bold, Italics always Italics, headings remain headings, and so on.

**HTML-Mail**   With ➠*e-mail* it is normally only possible to send plain text and not special characters (for example ü, ö, ä, ß, é, â, or ñ). ➠*HTML* not only solves this problem but it is also permits the use of text highlights (**bold**, *italic*, and so on), different colours, font sizes, images, backgrounds, headings, or lists in e-mails. On the one hand this is very useful, but on the other it is unfortunately not a generally accepted standard. Not every e-mail program can correctly display HTML mail, and not every recipient is glad to have such mail. HTML mail should only be used in exceptional cases and with the agreement of the recipient.

**HTTP**   Acronym for ➠*Hypertext Transfer Protocol*. Central ➠*protocol* that controls the structure of the data flow in the World Wide Web.

**Hypertext**   Neologism coined in the Sixties by Ted Nelson. Hypertext consists of several blocks of text that can be linked by almost any method, so that it is easy to switch between the blocks. A simple example for hypertext is the Office help texts. Individual terms are marked in the explanations. Clicking on the markings takes you to a different explanation, in which other terms are marked in turn. The entire structure of the ➠*World Wide Web* is based on this concept of linked information.

**IMAP**   Acronym for Internet Message Access Protocol; a new standard in the transmission of ➠e-mail. So far it is only rarely used.

**Importing**   When importing data, a file is opened in a different ➠*file format* and automatically converted into the format of the program. Example: opening a Lotus 1-2-3 table in Excel. ➠*Exporting*.

**Interface, graphical**   A graphical interface permits effortless access to all computer functions and programs. Usually it is the result of an attempt to simulate a normal office and desk environment with a bin, folders, and notes, in order to facilitate working with the computer.

**Internet**   World-wide network of millions of computers and networks. Nobody knows exactly how many linked computers there are. Current estimates (May 1999) talk of significantly more than 60 million connected systems. World-wide approximately 170 million people have access to the Internet and can exchange any data and information via the network. ➠*World Wide Web*.

**Intranet**   The techniques developed in the ➠*Internet* are also suitable to set up an inexpensive but powerful company network. Such a network is referred to as an Intranet.

**Junk-Mail**   Unwanted electronic mail, for example digital advertising is referred to as junk mail. ➠*Spam*.

**Kbyte**   The next bigger unit after ➠*byte*. It is often wrongly referred to as kilobyte. 'Kilo' however is a unit belonging to the decimal system and means a thousand times ($10^3$). One kilobyte would thus be equivalent to 1,000 ➠*bytes*. As a computer calculates with the ➠*binary system* this value is not correct, but too small. 1 Kbyte=1,024 bytes.

**Link**   Although Outlook internally works with ➠*folders*, these folders are not accessed directly. On the ➠*Outlook bar* there are different symbols which point to corresponding folders. This has the advantage that you can move, rename, or delete the symbols without actually physically changing the folder structure. This prevents the accidental deleting of folders. If you want to access the folders directly, you have to activate the ➠*folder list*.

**Linux**    A ➠*Unix* variant developed by Linus Torvalds. Linux is continually developed by a multitude of voluntary helpers and programmers. Today it is held to be the most powerful Unix for computers with a ➠*CPU* of Intel. Linux is freely distributed via the ➠*Internet*.

**Macintosh**    A computer brand of the company Apple. A Macintosh differs fundamentally from all other computer systems on the market. It possesses a separate ➠*operating system* and many ➠*hardware* peculiarities. Programs that run on a Macintosh cannot be used on Windows computers without special tools and vice versa.

**Mailbox**    Collecting point of your ➠*e-mail* on the ➠*server* of your ➠*provider* or your company network. The e-mail is stored in your mailbox until you download it to your computer by means of a mail program. The mailbox is secured by your personal ➠*password*. Everybody who knows your password can read your mail.

**Mailserver**    A program that deals with the transport and management of ➠*e-mail*, before you download it onto your computer with your mail program (➠*client*). There are two types of mail server: ➠*POP3* servers to manage your ➠*mailbox*, and ➠*SMTP* servers to transport the mail in the Internet.

**Mbyte**    The next bigger unit after ➠*Kbyte*. It is often wrongly referred to as megabyte. 'Mega' however is a unit belonging to the decimal system and means a million times ($10^3$). One megabyte would thus be equivalent to 1,000,000 ➠*bytes*. As a computer calculates with the ➠*binary system* this value is not correct, but too small. 1 Mbyte=1,024 ➠*Kbytes*=1,024*1,024 bytes=1,048,576 bytes.

**Menu**    In Windows menus are drop-down lists, via which you control all operations of a program. The individual menus are managed on the menu bar.

**Menu bar**    Central control element of a Windows program. It is almost always located at the top edge of a window. On the menu bar all sorts of commands are divided into groups such as 'File', 'Edit', or 'Format'. From there they can effortlessly be chosen with the mouse.

**MIME**    Acronym for Multipurpose Internet Mail Extensions. ➠*E-mail* can normally only send plain text without special characters. MIME is a special procedure to remove this restriction. A prerequisite is, however, that the sender and the recipient use a MIME-capable e-mail program. Current programs are almost always MIME-capable.

**Moving**   Developed from ➠*copying*. The file to be moved is first copied to a new location, and then the original is deleted.

**Operating system**   Basic ➠*Software*, without which a computer cannot work. The operating system controls the central input and output functions of a computer and, for example, ensures that when you press a key the corresponding letter appears on your screen or that a file can be saved. The operating system is the mediating program between the actual application (text processing, appointment planner, game ...) and the ➠*hardware* of the computer.

**Outlook database**   Outlook stores all entries in a single database, which is usually called 'outlook.pst' and is located in the Windows directory under *Microsoft/Application Data/Outlook*. It is easily possible to create several Outlook databases and open these simultaneously, for example, for the archiving of folders and entries.

**Outlook bar**   On the Outlook bar are ➠*links* that point to the corresponding ➠*folders*. In Outlook the folders are normally accessed via the Outlook bar. To directly access folders the ➠*folder list* is used.

**Password**   A password is a code word with which you prevent unauthorised access to your ➠*mailbox*. It is the key to your mailbox and thus has to be treated with care, just like the key to a safety deposit box: Do not disclose it to strangers, do not forget it, and store it in a secure place. Always remember that everybody who has your password can read your mail and can send mail messages in your name.

**POP3**   Acronym for Post Office Protocol, Version 3, a special procedure for ➠*e-mail* management. POP3 ensures that your mail ends up in your ➠*mailbox*, which can only be opened with your ➠*password*.

**Protocol**   To make it possible for two computers to exchange data, it has to be ensured that they can understand each other. When one computer sends an 'x', the other cannot receive a 'u'. In a so-called protocol the behaviour according to which certain data have to be send is exactly described. There are many different protocols. The two most important are  ➠*POP3* and ➠*SMTP*.

**Provider**    A provider offers you access to the ➡*Internet*.

**Quoted Printable**    One of several coding options which has established itself as a *de facto* standard and which permits special characters with ➡*MIME* in ➡*e-mails*.

**Rich Text Format**    Special ➡*file format* that permits text highlights such as **bold**, italic, and <u>underline</u> or various font sizes across different platforms. File extension: .rtf. A range of programs can process RTF files without problems. However, it is not recommended as a format for ➡*e-mail*, as not every mail program can work with it.

**Series (appointments and tasks)**    Outlook refers to recurring appointments or tasks, such as 'every Monday at 10:00 conference' or 'create a backup copy every 3 days' as series.

**Server**    Counterpart to ➡*client*. A server provides different functions and services, which can be accessed by a suitable client. A server is actually a special type of ➡*software*. However, as usually a single computer works with this software, the computer itself, that is the ➡*hardware*, is often referred to as server, too. A network works with the client-server model, in which the server represents the central instance that can be accessed by various client machines. In this way ➡*e-mail* is transported via mail servers and managed, read, and processed by mail clients (that is mail programs such as Outlook Express).

**SMTP**    Acronym for Simple Mail Transfer Protocol (➡*protocol*). SMTP defines by which method ➡*e-mail* is forwarded from ➡*server* to server on the ➡*Internet*. Only the transportation of the plain letters and numbers is defined, but not that of special characters. To be able to use special characters a coding of the mail with ➡*MIME* and ➡*quoted printable* is necessary.

**Software**    Everything on a computer that exists but cannot be touched. The memory unit you can touch is ➡*hardware*; in contrast the program which exists in form of electronic pulses in the memory unit is referred to as software.

**Spam**    Spam is the common term for ➡*junk mail* on the net. It is actually the brand name of tinned meat produced by the US company Hormel. It is not absolutely clear how the term has been coined, however, there is a strong indication which points to a sketch of the same name by the English comedy team Monty Python. In this sketch a conversation is jeopardised by the continual nonsensical repetition of the word 'Spam'. In the same way junk mail jeopardises the useful application of the e-mail system.

**Status bar**   A text bar at the bottom edge of the window of many windows programs. Here a range of specifications concerning the current status of the program is displayed.

**Toolbar**   In many Windows programs a bar containing different symbols with which program functions that are difficult to reach via the menu bar can be called up directly. The toolbar can usually be placed freely on the screen.

**Unix**   One of the most important ➠*operating systems* on the ➠*Internet*. There are different Unix variants. One of the most important variants is ➠*Linux*.

**Uploading**   Opposite of ➠*downloading*.

**URL**   Acronym for Uniform Resource Locator (also referred to as Internet address). It states the exact location of a file on a computer on the world-wide ➠*Internet*.

**Virus**   A virus is a small program that is able to reproduce itself. In almost all cases viruses are destructive programs which wipe out data. Usually a virus attaches itself inconspicuously to another program. As soon as this program is started it is activated. Viruses can be extremely dangerous and cause irreparable damage. Protect yourself from viruses by regularly running an anti-virus software.

**Web address**   The ➠*Internet* address of a ➠*Web page* defines the exact location of a Web page on a specific computer on the ➠*World Wide Web*.

**Web page**   An ➠*HTML* file which is displayed on your screen by a ➠*browser*.

**Windows**   This Microsoft program is the most widely distributed ➠*operating system* for computers with an *Intel* ➠*CPU*.

**World Wide Web**   The World Wide Web (abbreviated: WWW) is a part of the ➠*Internet* and by now so huge and important that in almost all cases when the Internet is mentioned the WWW is meant. The World Wide Web permits the linking of different information and its graphical representation in interactive form. It is so to speak a graphical ➠*interface* for the Internet.

**317**